Creative Design for Home

A Collection of Creative Furniture and Household Items

ARTPOWER

Creative Design for Home

— A Collection of Creative Furniture and Household Items

Copyright © Artpower International Publishing Co., Ltd.

ARTPOWER

Publisher: Lu Jican
Chief Editor: Li Aihong
Executive Editor: Li Aihong
Art Designer: Xiong Libo
Registered Address
Suites 2001, 20/F., Chinachem Tower, 36 Connaught Road Central, Hong Kong, China
Tel: 852-31840676
Fax: 852-25432396

Editorial Department
Address: G009, Floor 7th, Yimao Centre, Meiyuan Road, Luohu District, Shenzhen, China
Tel: 86-755-25111140
Fax: 86-755-82020029

Web: www.artpower.com.cn / www.acs.cn
Sales & Distribution: overseasales@artpower.com.cn
Press & Editorial Submissions: press@artpower.com.cn / contact@artpower.com.cn

ISBN 978-988-19982-1-7

No part of this publication may be reproduced or utilised in any form by any means, electronic or mechanical, including photocopying, recording or by any information storage and retrieval system, without prior written permission of the publisher.

All images in this book have been reproduced with the knowledge and prior consent of the designers and the clients concerned, and every effort has been made to ensure that credits accurately comply with information applied. No responsibility is accepted by producer, publisher, or printer for any infringement of copyright or otherwise arising from the contents of this publication.

Printed and Bound in China.

CONTENTS

006

Accessories

028

Lamps

072

Cabinets & Bookshelves

088

Tables & Chairs & Sofa

150

Kitchenware & Containers

184

Tools

202

Children's Furniture

Accessories

273 Collection

Water is one of the few substances in nature in which the process of solidification has an increase of specific volume.

We have created, thanks to the experience of "De Vecchi Milano 1935, a series of silver vases which form depends by water expansion inside them, when putted at 273 ° k, or 0 ° c.

Each piece of the collection, which form can not be designed but comes itself, is so unique even if following all the same process.

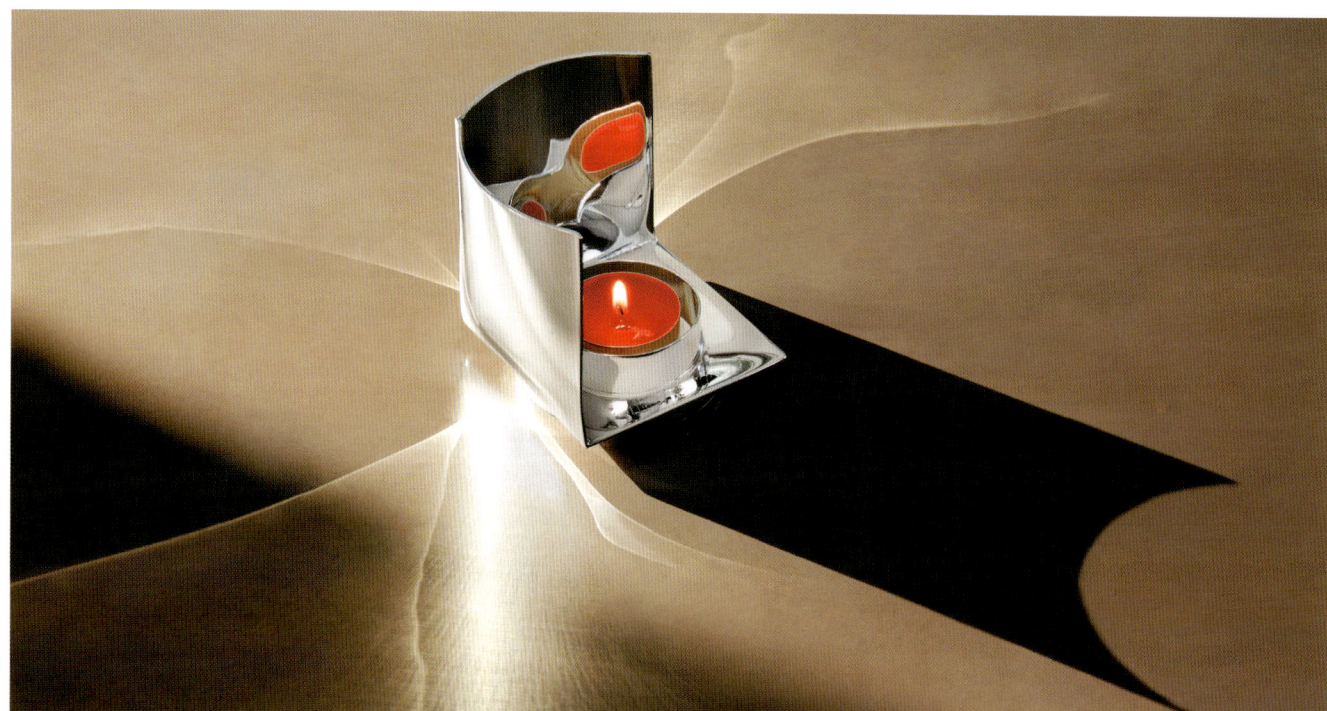

Designer: 4P1B Design Studio and Antonio de Marco
Material: Silver-plated brass

Client: De Vecchi Milano 1935 (Milan)

DEUS Collection

DEUS is a couple of objects turned into machines by 4P1B. The brass structure is actually a mechanism that allows the object to be used. The pitcher can be tilted to pour its content, the candle holder can turn off the flame by pulling a lever that shuts down the oxigen income.

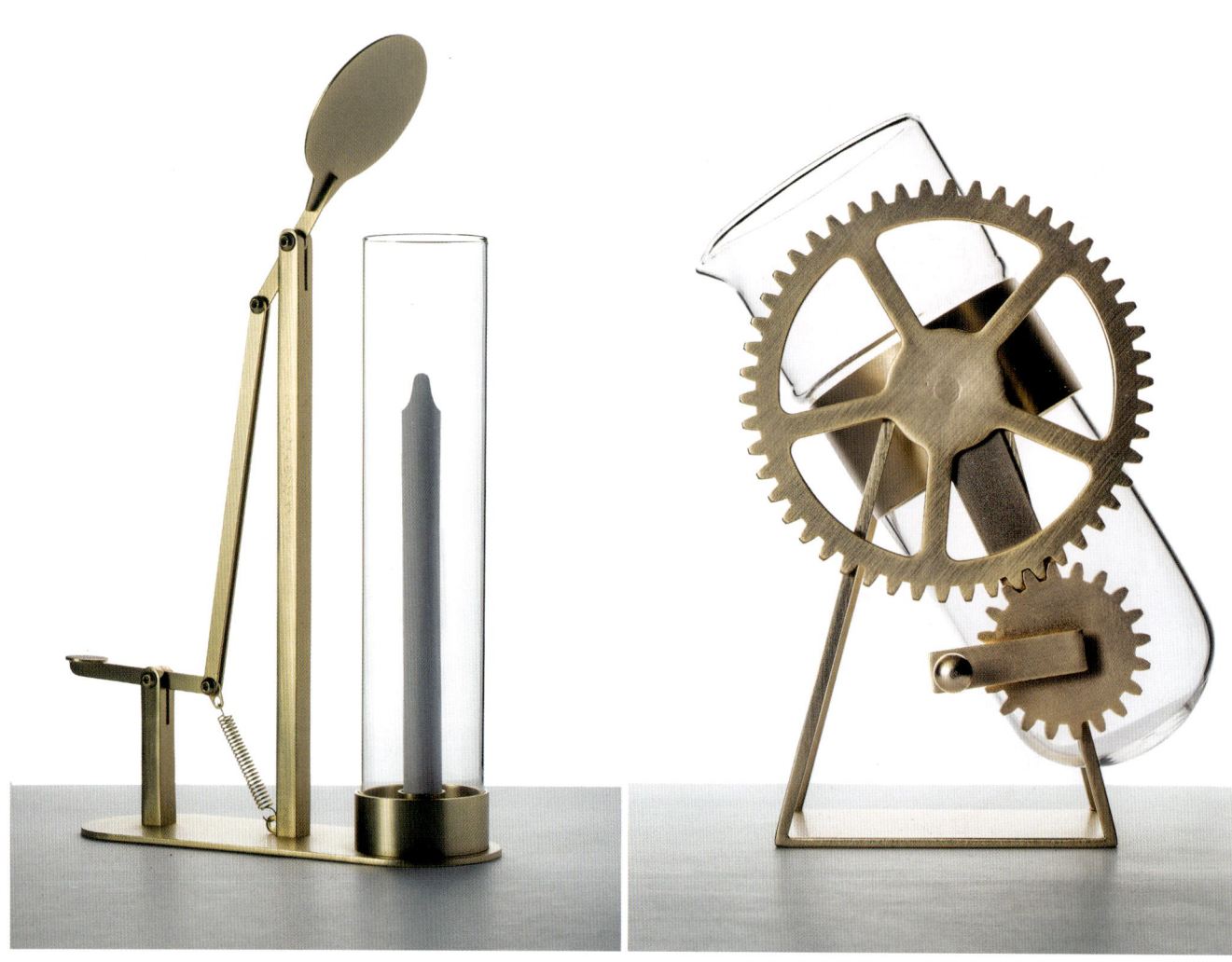

Designer: 4P1B Design Studio and Antonio de Marco
Material: Brass and glass

Client: Secondome Gallery (Rome)

Juice

Juice is a basket made of leather or rubber. Juice's tetrahedral shape takes inspiration from paper packagings in which one of the edges is cut in order to pour the content. The large and strong body can be easily moved thanks to a handle. Juice is available in 100% leather or in an unusual rubber version, which is water resistant and is provided with leather handles.

Designer: 4P1B Design Studio and Antonio de Marco
Material: Leather or Rubber

Client: Edizione Limitata

Revolution

Three mirrors with a clean and rigorous design consisting of identical elements that are mounted at different angles to obtain various configurations. The result is a light balance between frames, mirrors and wall.

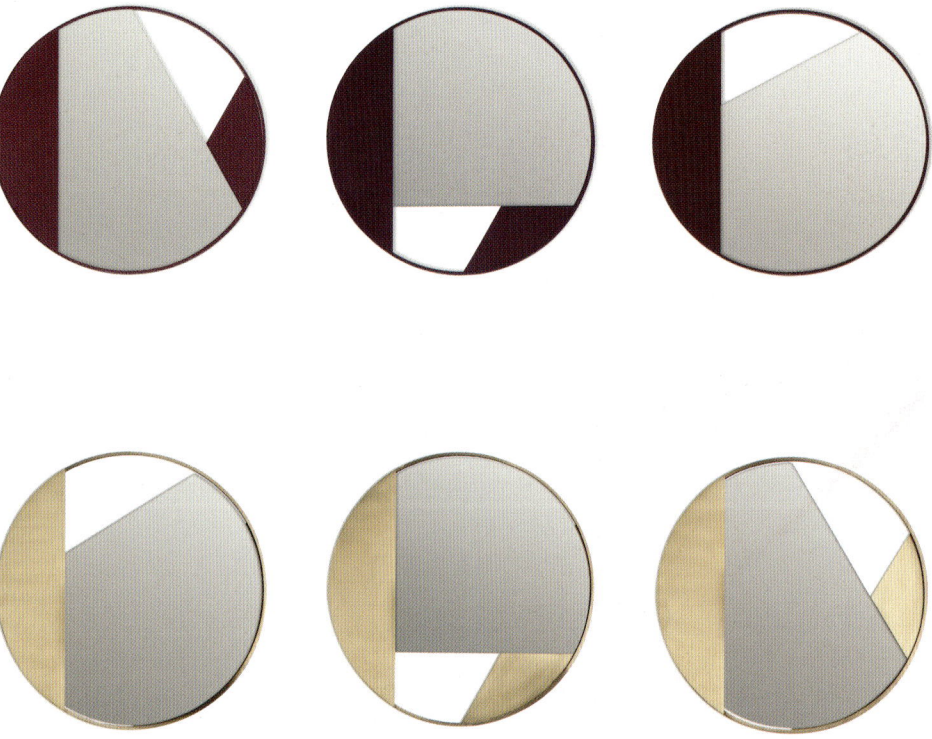

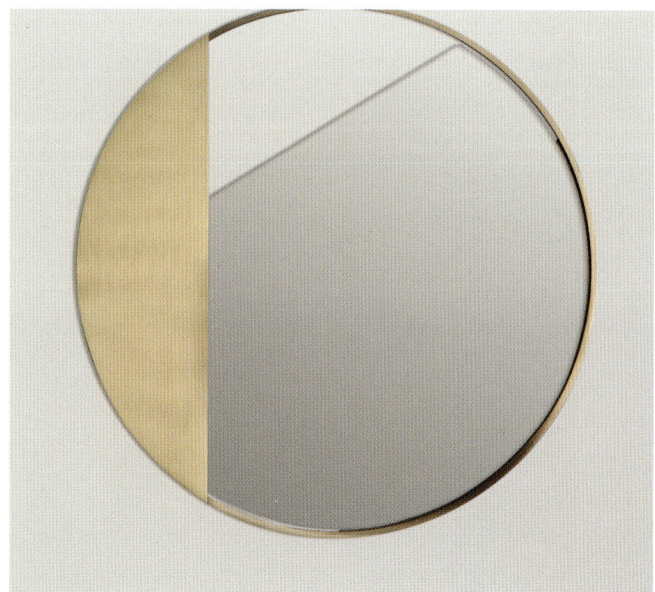

Design Studio: 4P1B Design Studio, Antonio de Marco and Carolina Becatti
Material: Painted Metal or Brass

Client: Edizone Limitata

Concavo Convesso Collection (Volcano)

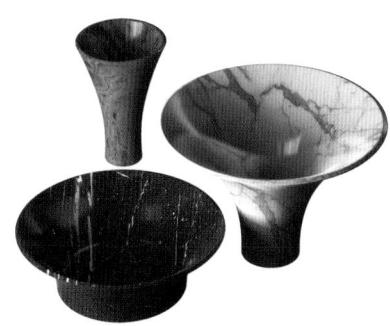

Designer: Massimo Iosa Ghini
Company: Guarda Marbles & Stones Srl

Lume

The fabled brilliance of the night of St. Lucia; the awesome spectacle of San Lorenzo, night of the shooting stars; the power of the magic lamp in the Arabian Nights; and the hypnotic gleam of the pearl earring in the painting by Vermeer: all are celebrations of light.

With its innate splendour, wonder and expectation, light has the power to alter space. It takes us by surprise and fires the imagination. Light, indeed, is the glowing heart of "Lume", the new project by Alessandro Zambelli for Bosa.

Designer: Alessandro Zambelli

SELFPORTRAIT hand mirror

The item inspired by the oriental fans proposes the mirror as a feminine accessory symbol of luxury and beauty. The lightness and harmony of the wrinkles of paper fans are impressed in the wood through the work of an expert Italian carver.

Designer: Ilaria Innocenti & Giorgio Laboratore
Photography: Hyphen-Italia

Concave Metamorphosis Mirror

The Concave Metamorphosis Mirror portrays a territorial dispute, where chaos is indulged and spread across simplicity represented by the clean slate upon which it takes place. A take on metamorphosis from both its literal and philosophical meaning, this luxurious mirror represents the removal of creative boundaries, and tests the beauty ideal.

Materials and Finishes

The Concave Metamorphosis Mirror is made from brass. It is hand hammered to shape, coated in a nickel bath. The insects are also cast from brass, and undergo a chemical treatment for finish.

Design Studio: Boca do Lobo
Arts and Techniques: Metal cutting, foudry, welding, polishing

Metamorphosis

By definition, metamorphosis indicates an alteration is physical build and structure, commonly associated with insects. As a great novel of the 20th Century, written by a phenomenal thinker for his time, Franz Kafka, Metamorphosis digs deep introspection, unknowingly looking for meaning or something to hang on to.

This is the word which rung in conversation and thought, and has come to symbolize a new line of thought, and design inspiration for Boca do Lobo.

Design Studio: Boca do Lobo

Robin Mirror

From the legend born in the depths of Sherwood Forest, ROBIN Mirror embodies the strength and character of noble ages, giving them a modern approach. By honoring the history of one of the best archers in English literature, this exquisite piece was given a strong visual texture through the use of handmade nails, each one unique in their finishing, size and character. The fish-eye mirror is supported by a brass structure that turns ROBIN into one of the most emblematic pieces of the entire collection.

Product features: Set of hand-made brass nails with hand-made textures applied. Brass structure and fish-eye mirror.

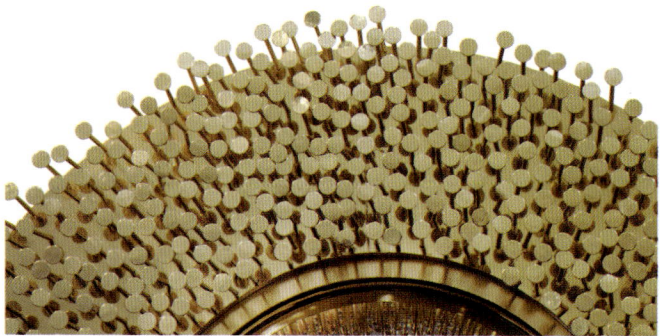

Design Studio: Boca do Lobo
Arts and Techniques: Jewellery techniques

Materials and Finishes: Polished Brass with hand-made engraved texture

Barlume

Barlume is a collection of glass candle holders inspired by the most classic and iconic object of Italian tables and osterias. The stylised bottle comes in a contrast combination of metal finishes and delicate transparent colours, which range from gray to light blue to fuchsia, applied using the ancient luster varnish technique of the Venetian glassmakers. A minimal yet precious decoration for a romantic atmosphere.

Designer: Filippo Castellani
Client: INCIPIT LAB

Phantom for Smaller Objects

In French the term 'vide-poche' is used for a small container - in your entry hall or at bedside - where to put your keys, small change etcetera.

What would be lightest way to provide this; to make your small valuables lightly float in suspension before returning to your pocket next day?

Originally, the technique of heat pressing polyester mesh was used for producing oil filters of car engines. When designer Jin Kuramoto met the Japanese manufacture NBC Meshtech Inc. they used the same technology to supply the quality industry with a product for sifting wheat flour.

"I was intrigued by the beauty. I really saw some design possibilities in this up-until-now solely industrial product," says Kuramoto.

Together with the manufacture he researched and developed a bowl that would use the least amount of material, yet be rigid enough to hold the weight. The result is a vide-poche, which appears almost non-material; like a phantom.

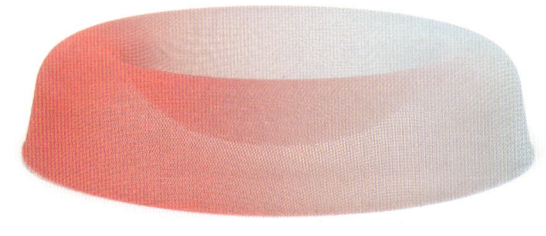

Designer: Jin Kuramoto
Material: polyester mesh

Photography: Jin Kuramoto Studio

WIND for OFFECCT

These room dividers are a concept more than individual products. They can be seen as a celebration of the beauty of nature — a forest of organic shapes that also control acoustics like a kind of tuner, and that make the environment more pleasant and friendly. My inspiration always comes from nature.

There are no more perfects shapes than those of a snowflake, a bee hide or a leaf. I think that it will be very nice to have these room dividers as reminders of nature's beauty in a hospital or a large office landscape, for example. They also make it possible to speak in private even in acoustically chaotic environments.

Designer: Jin Kuramoto
photography: OFFECCT

Off The Moon

Off The Moon collection is a complete family of four trays, two standing trays and four side tables that have been designed by Thomas Dariel. With these ten pieces, he proposes us a journey around the Moon and its inherent poetry.

From earth, one can only see the portion of the moon that is illuminated by the sun. An image that is constantly changing as the moon orbits the Earth. The collection draws its inspiration from this fascinating connectivity.

Designer: Thomas Dariel

Paris-Memphis

Paris-Memphis capsule collection consists of nine original pieces of candleholders. Thomas Dariel draws its inspiration and pays homage to The Memphis Design Movement created in 1981 by Ettore Sottsass.

Unstructured shapes and asymmetric lines bring humour, energy and flamboyance to the entire series.

While N.6 and N.7 candleholders feature bold indigo blue colour rather alluding to pop art, the rest of the collection - with pastel tones and delicate shades of champagne, copper and pink-copper metal finish – further remind the Art Deco geometrical elegancy.

Designer: Thomas Dariel

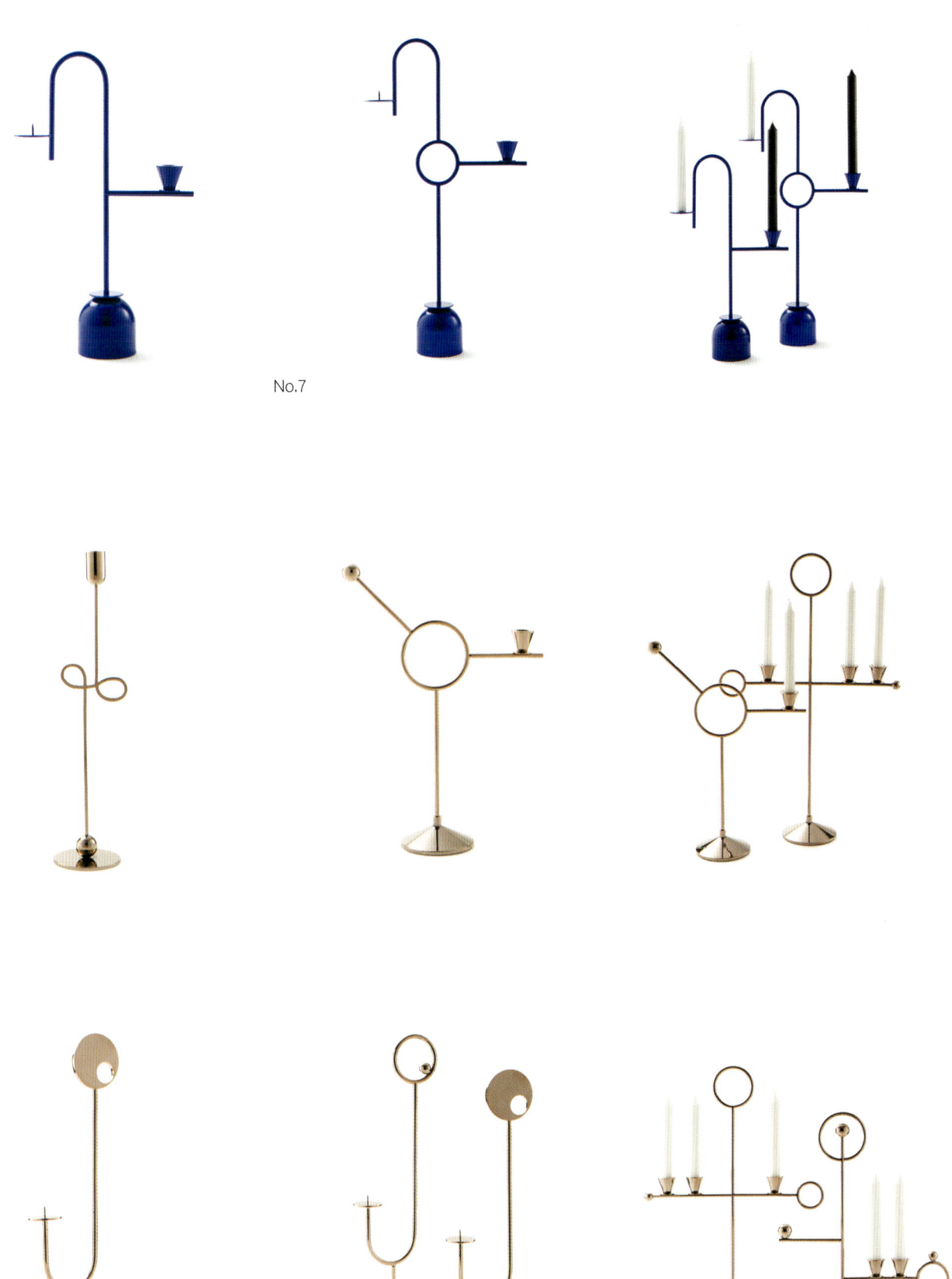

No.6 No.7

Collezione Sospesa_Marble Vases

ENG_Nowadays the carrara white marble is considered more and more to be sold per ton than ever before. Usually the blocks are covered with resin to increase the stress resistance imparted by the cutting machine used to obtain slabs (2-3 cm thickness). The collection designed for the "MarmoTrilogy" has been inspired by this process with the intention to emphasize the material and the artisan know-how to obtain unique and not replicable objects.

The marble pieces are achieved by using waste material coming from coring. The resin symbolizes the discarded material (spectrum) that a careless use would take to produce the same marble piece.

Designer: Moreno Ratti
Material: Marmo di Carrara + Resin

Candles

Tribute candles that invite to think over what happened.

Design Firm/Designer: Nueve estudio
Client: Self-initiated
Materials: Wax
Photography: Caterina Barjau

Lamps

Reverb

In times past, in an autumn dawn, winter peeped from a distance at five friends, who were silently scaling the precipitous slopes of Mount Borgà. "The early morning light inched its way along the village rooftops. The frost glistened like icing sugar on the cobbles of the steep and winding streets. The men used carbide lamps to light the way ahead…" All the experience of life in the raw from Mauro Corona's mountain tales is embodied in Reverb, the new design by Alessandro Zambelli for Zava: a collection of desk lamps inspired by the carbide lanterns of olden times.

A keynote feature of the product line is a concave diffuser with circular screen, supported on a cylindrical base. Like a little illuminating dish, Reverb radiates its light outwards into space, bathing its surroundings in warm, luminous reflections. The all-metal collection is available in carmine red, pastel turquoise and grey beige colour options, and accommodates LED light sources.

Designer: Alessandro Zambelli

Quayside Pendant Light

The Quayside Light, draws inspiration from the simplicity and functionality of industrial pendant lights of a bygone era.

Constructed from spun aluminium, the Quayside Light is available in 5 different colours: yellow, white, black, red and grey with a corresponding coloured fabric braided cable.

With its elegant outline and its two tone colour scheme (coloured exterior, white interior) this large contemporary classic pendent light will have an impact on any room.

Design Firm: Assemblyroom
Designer: Peter Wall

PET Lamp

In 2011, Alvaro Catalán de Ocón took part in a project focused on the reuse of PET plastic bottles. He addressed the plastic waste issue in the Colombian Amazon by turning a short lifespan object –PET plastic bottles– into a product enriched by the local culture –a lamp weaved with the local textile tradition–. PET Lamp believes in the reuse as the counterpoint of recycling. Collaborating with artisans from the Cauca region displaced by the guerrilla war and using traditional crafts and materials the PET Lamp Project was founded. In 2012 the Colombian experience was launched with the Eperara-Siapidara collection. In 2013 it expanded to Chile with the Chimbarongo collection made by wicker artisans. In 2015 Alvaro's Catalan de Ocón PETLamp Project broadens its horizons. A whole new continent, Africa, becomes a new part of the project. Focusing in the basket weaving tradition of Ethiopían artisans we have developed with them our new PETLamp collection Abyssinia.

Designer: Alvaro Catalan de Ocon
Manufacturer: ACdO

Photography: PET Lamp in Vitra Haus, 2013 by Lorenz Cugini Concept

Streamlined Light

The Streamlined collection reflects the true character of the everyday material of plywood. Due to its structural value, plywood usually serves a purely functional purpose. "A real shame", says Studio Roex, "because its multiple layers of bonded wood veneer are what make it so unique".

Streamlined aims to reveal the true identity of plywood by emphasizing the various wood layers that are usually only marginally visible. By CNC milling the two-dimensional plywood sheet material, a three-dimensional material can be produced. As a result, the pattern of layers flares out, creating a subtle interplay of lines.

Design Studio: Studio Roex

HAMMER lamp for Wiener Silber Manufactur

The collaboration with Wiener Silber Manufactur was an opportunity for BIG-GAME to explore the hand crafting of precious materials.

Upon visiting the workshop, we realized that each piece produced there is a small treasure, and we wanted to create a functional object that would celebrate the beauty of the craft but at the same time have a contemporary expression.

Designer: BIG-GAME

SMALLWORK for Habitat

SMALLWORK is a compact minimal table lamp.

Light, functional and stable with its tripod shape, it is made from anodized aluminium profiles with integrated LED's for optimal lighting.

It is sold in a tubular packaging and is easily assembled by connecting the two feet to the body of the lamp.

Available from Habitat from October 2015.

Designer: BIG-GAME

Ann Floor Lamp

Ann is a contemporary floor lamp composed by a minimal modern structure with a perfectly matching square lampshade. The lampshade is sized to balance the architectural form and is available either in fabric or silk. This floor lamp is a magnificent modern light and it is suited for any quiet place of your home.

Product features:
Floor lamp supported by a stainless steel structure.

Design Studio: Boca do Lobo
Arts and Techniques: Carpentry, Varnishing and Electricity

Union Table Lamp

Handcrafted by Boca do Lobo, Union is an exclusive lamp created by using the traditional techniques of joinery and then finished with lacquer. The lacquer finish is available in two colors (white or black). Highly decorative, the form and design is achieved by working in turn of the piece. The lamp's base can be made from solid oak wood, beech tree or mahogany that makes the subsequent work of shaping possible. The lampshade is available in either fabric or silk.

Design Studio: Boca do Lobo

Silhouette

This family of pendant lamps is inspired by the traditional construction of the lampshades for the scattering of light: a structure in metallic wire where is wound a tissue. But in this case the idea is to flip the concept: what was hidden and was serving only as support, the metal structure, it's now highlighted, and it's given a greater value and elegance by producing it with borosilicate glass rods welded together, while eliminating the fabric. This creates many small silhouettes, almost a kind of "glass sketches", enhanced by the reflections generated by the light source.

Designer: Giorgio Bonaguro
Design Firm: selfproduction
Material: borosilicate glass

Client: Mercado Moderno Gallery (Rio de Janeiro, Brazil)
Photographer: Andrea Basile Studio

Endless

Endless started out of a fascination to create a container for the future. Followed by wanting to show the endlessness of the future, and giving people the possibility to place themselves in this endlessness, and create a place to stare in and dream.

People can start to invent their own future, and escape their busy environments for a while. Endless is a portal to wander, a place where people can find the time to get lost.

This resulted in a series of lamps/mirrors, in 3 different sizes, with a movable translucent mirror. The movement of the mirror creates different endless light patterns, and makes you look in to the infinity, or place yourself into it. Lamp shapes are casted in resin and have different colors by the influence of light according to their translucency.

 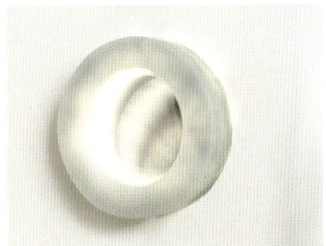 

Designer: Bram Vanderbeke
Materials: Polyester Resin, Acrylic Mirror, Translucent Acrylic Mirror, Tridonic LED Lights

Atomic Round Lamp

With a contemporary descendant of retro sphere lighting, this piece is a unique spot-on interpretation of the atomic age design. Compound in a set of brilliant black shades and gold plated spun brass. Atomic creation is made of an asymmetric composition to enhance non-conventional molecular forms. It is the perfect design invention to be placed in a living room (or even dining room) and involve your guests in a modern lobby. Make them feel like they are in another galaxy!

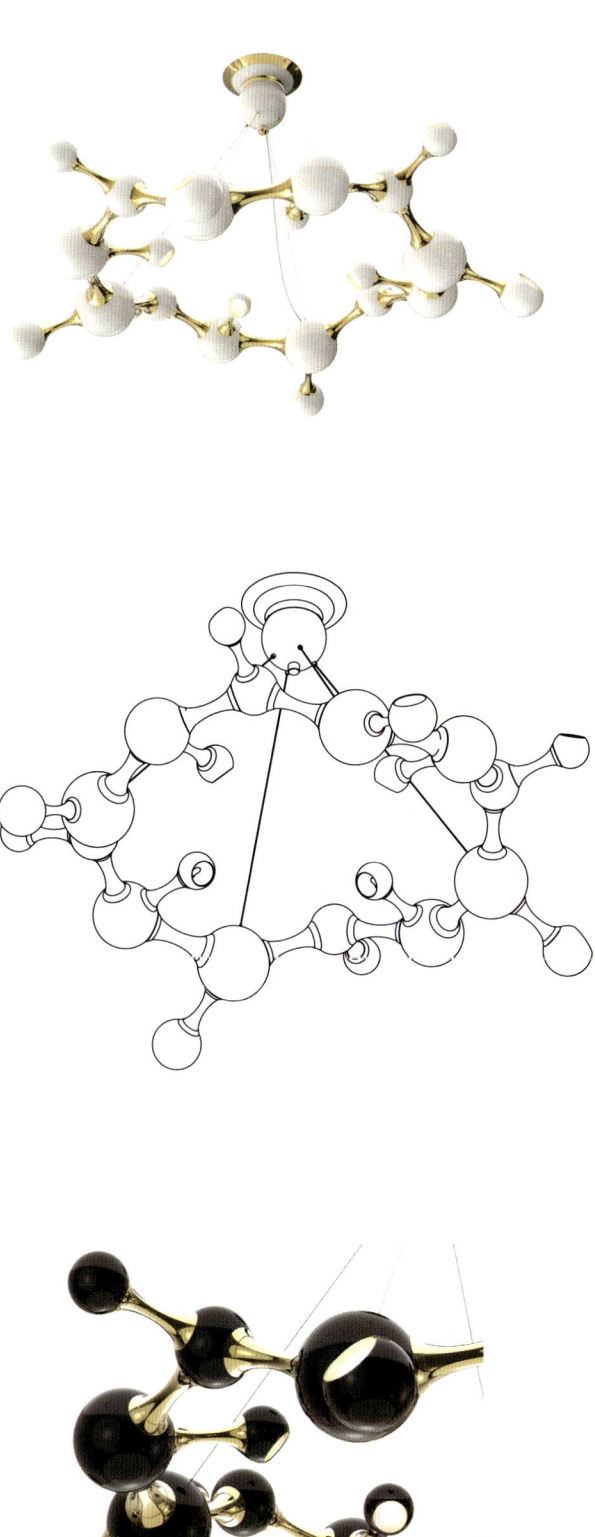

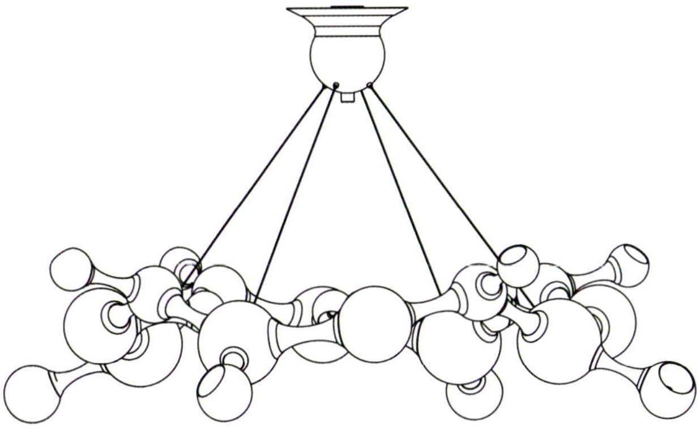

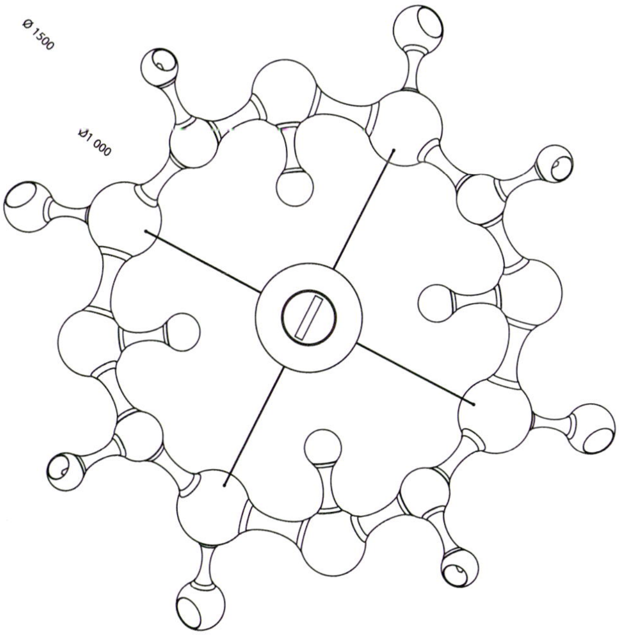

Botti Collection

Like an orchestra, Botti embodies all the details of wind instruments and takes us into a music concert. Its structure is handmade in brass and gently covered by a golden mantle, a monumental piece which shows the exquisite capacity of Delightfull's skilled artisans. Botti Table will surely mark a 'before' and 'after' in any setting.

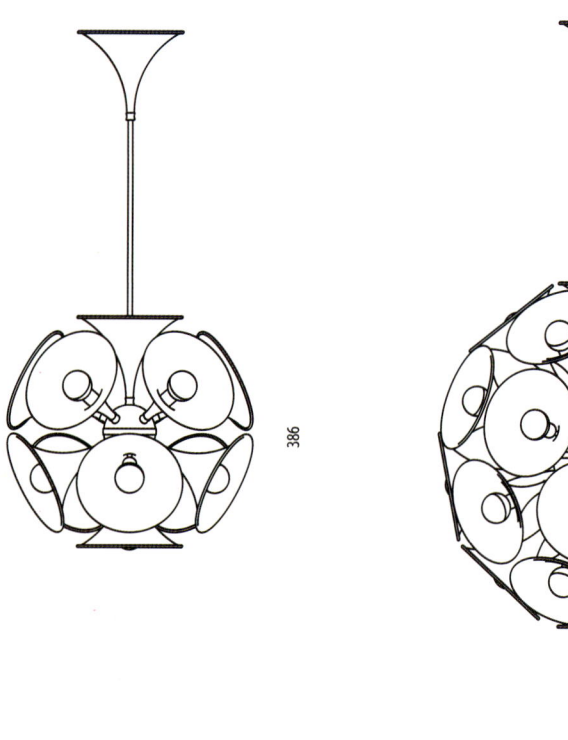

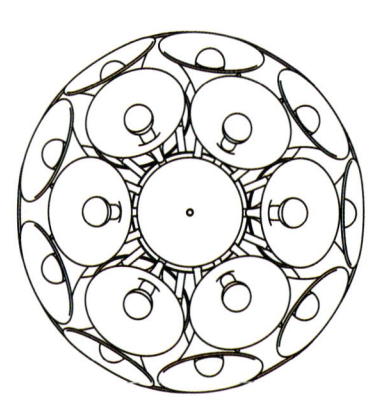

Design Studio: DelightFULL
Materials: Nero Marquina and Brass

Donna Table Lamp

Donna Lee was the eye candy jazz tune, fast moving and every little bit complex. Inspired by this beautiful composition, DelightFULL designers have created the most noble and elegant of light fixtures, the Donna Table Lamp.

This noble and elegant piece boasts a patterned composition of straight brass tubes in rhythm with the irregular shades of the Carrara white marble, defining the jazzy saxophone melody creating a beautiful match for the classiest environments. The warm light passing through the golden tubes makes every sitting room cozy and charming sending you on a journey to the long gone golden decades.

Design Studio: DelightFULL
Materials: Brass

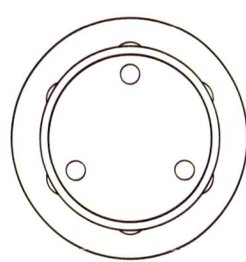

Ø 244

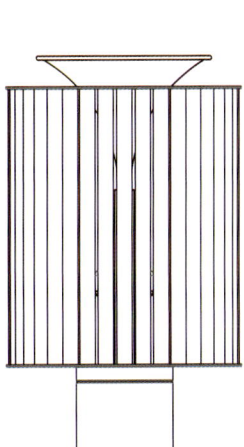

689

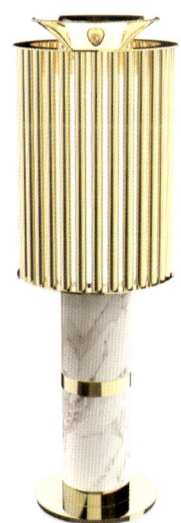

Ø 187

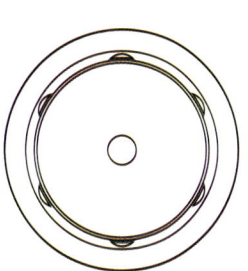

Etta Round Lamp

Perfect for a living room or even just a relaxing corner, this unique design invention brings luxury and a refined art touch for any place.

Inspired by the jazz singer Etta Jones, Etta Round Lamp has a nostalgic and feminine retro glow. This opulent chandelier can provide a soft and warm light through its layers, offering a romantic atmosphere to any setting. All brass leafs are shaped and assembled by our artisans' hands, bended using manual molds, an old Portuguese technique that is part of DelightFULL's mission to preserve.

Following the lighting essence with an alternative conception, our stupendous team of designers decided to create something different. From the iconic design they created a new piece ready for a lot of project design solutions has huge dining tables, chic hotel lobbys, or even restaurants.

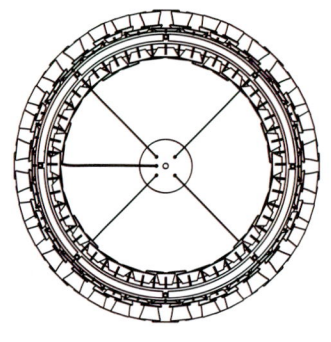
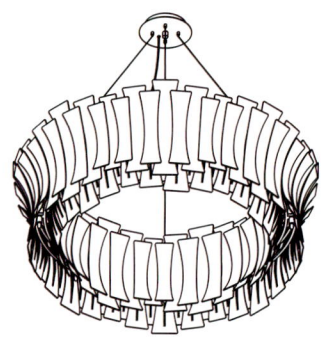
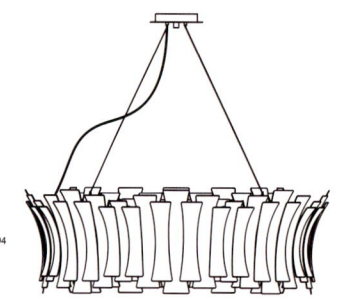

Design Studio: DelightFULL
Materials: Brass

Hendrix Suspension

Hendrix is another rich addition to DelightFULL core Heritage Collection.

Heritage is a collection of retro inspired lamps based in the most iconic creations of the 40's and 50's era. And not only jazz but rock legends from the past move and inspired DelightFULL studio to create masterpieces of lighting.

Heritage has almost 90 pieces of lighting within its collection and it's growing.

The range of it is complete by the Suspension, Floor, Table and Wall lighting as well as exquisite lamps design ready for and outdoor use like the Galliano wall light and the Coltrane wall lamp which was an and still is one of the best seller pieces of DelightFULL brand.

Design Studio: DelightFULL
Materials: Brass

○ A Collection of Creative Furniture and Household   047

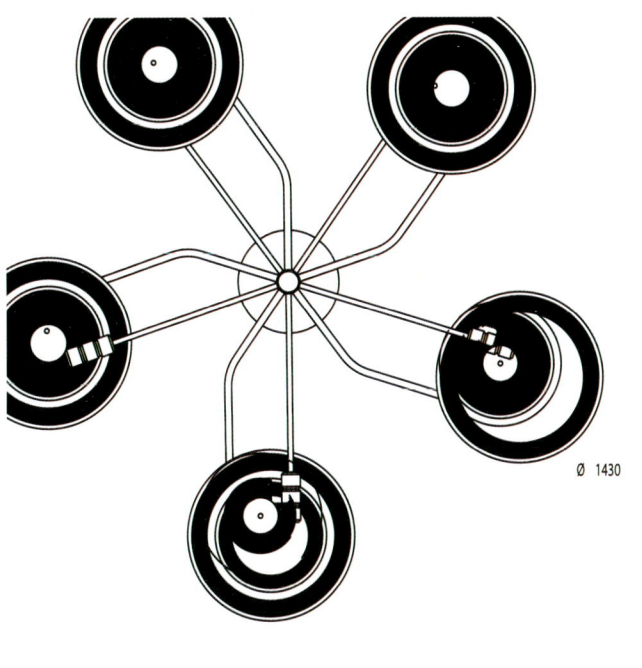

Ø 1430

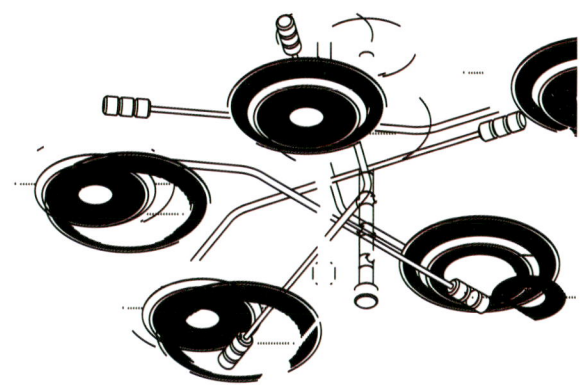

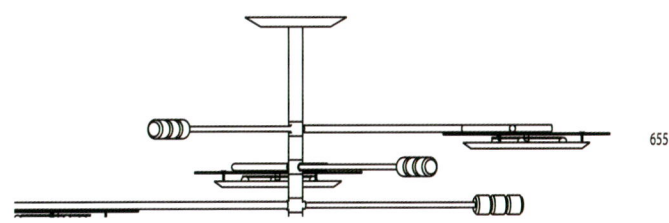

655

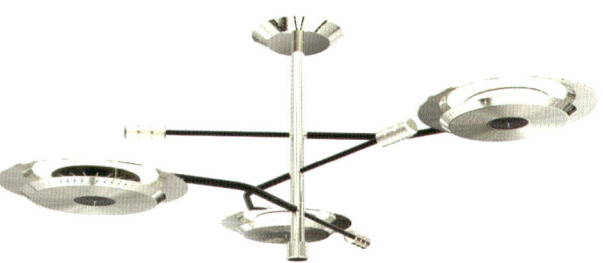

Bolet Wire

Bolet wire is an evolution of our popular Bolet pendants. The stainless steel frames follow the original silhouette, now with a wire frame construction.

Finishes include polished stainless steel or electroplated copper, brass and pearl black. Powder coat options include black, white or custom colours POA.

This beautiful and refined collection comes in a variety of sizes and looks remarkable hanging in a continuous line or cluster.

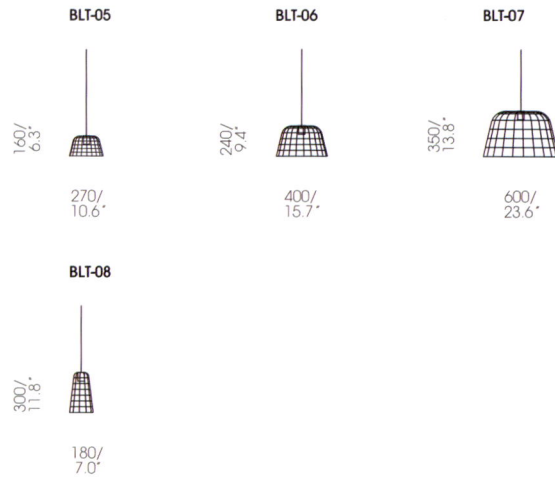

Designer: Alexander Lotersztain
Material: Pendant Stainless Steel

Photographer: Florian Groehn

Mirror Mobiles

ELKELAND is a visual studio, which resides in a sancturay situated deep in the danish countryside.

Her work translates the experience of falling into a reverie, to visual objects for unconventional homes.

Designer: Ida Elke Kallehave

KALIKA

Table lamp inspired by the shapes of nature: hence its name, KALIKA, which means "bud" in Hindi, with a strong and lush character, born to blossom and give life to a sophisticated lighting.

KALIKA, born from the recent collaboration of Massimo Iosa Ghini with Venini, is enriched with a lampshade finely manufactured by master glassmakers Venini.

The central diffuser is made of blown Murano glass in colored crystal and hides an hi-tech light source with LED strip light of 15 watts.

The lampshade, in colored crystal as the diffuser, is made with a unique blown mold and a rigadìn effect with vertical stripes, which refract the light in a myriad of shades and ripples, like the quiet waves of Murano canals.

The base and the central stem of the lamp are available in two versions: one in metal and the other is enhanced by a cone-shaped blown glass, rigadin worked harmonized with the lampshade.

A light and soft design with the intrinsic qualities of Venini production.

Designer: Massimo Iosa Ghini
Company: Venini

PIN

Japanese designer Ichiro Iwasaki explores ideas connected with continuity and comfort through this collection of lamps for VIBIA. The PIN collection is conceived as a new interpretation on the ambient and task lighting lamp perfectly compatible with both traditional and contemporary interior spaces.

Designer: Fitcut Curve

Cubo Light

Cubo is a sustainable light using low voltage LED source, made from FSC beech wood finished with Danish oil. Cubo is an extension to the Blocks range, a small light performing soft warm white spot light. The playful front metal ring comes in a selection of different colours. Thanks to this, the Cubo can fit in different interiors such as children's rooms, living rooms, working areas and so on.

Cubo is designed to be hung onto the wall - the light can be pointing upwards, downwards or even at an angle. It can be placed on a table, a shelve and even on the floor. It is safe to the touch and will fit into your hand palm.

Designer: Rona Meyuchas-Koblenz, Kukka Studio
Material: Hand Crafter FSC Beech wood

Felucca Large

Felucca© is a simple lampshade made from non-woven flame-proof Nomex fabric and snap fasteners, to be mounted directly onto a suspended light bulb.

It can then be shaped gently by hand, and several Feluccas can also be assembled to create a larger lampshade. Once mounted, The Felucca casts a soft, smooth and elegant light.

Designer: Rona Meyuchas K.

Fungo Chandelier

The Fungo chandelier was inspired by the fascinating shape of a mushroom growing on wood. Yet this mushroom didn't grow in the forest, but was discovered in the basement of Lasvit's glassworks, where an ancient wooden glassblowing mold had succumbed to the ravages of humidity. The Campana brothers chose to blend this newfound accidental theme with Lasvit's glassmaking tradition and fuse their techniques with natural materials. The resulting artwork displays a striking contrast between the formal rigidity of the chandelier's wooden structure and the blown-glass that appears to emerge spontaneously from the wood.

Designer: Campana Brothers

Giffy Lamp

The shape for the Giffy concept was inspired by a photo picturing giraffes standing majestically next to Acacia trees in a beautiful savannah sunset– a sight that represents very well the diversity, beauty and functionality that is so characteristic of nature.

Designer: Markus Oder of Leanter

ENDLESS Light

This Japanese-style organic Voronoi cellular structure light is Made of laser cut Plywood. It creates many beautiful shadows creating romantic, intimate atmosphere. Design represent minimalist and clean aesthetics from nature.

Designer: Mariam Ayvazyan

Sun Green Chandelier

Sun green chandelier by made in love design studio is unique light, a result of one year of experiments with materials and shapes. It's entirely designed and handcrafted by mariam ayvazyan.

The chandelier consists of 88 handmade concrete eggs and an edison bulbs in the middle. Inside each egg, there is carefully placed led light. Groups of four eggs are attached by brass wire rings. The origami wooden base that is attached to the ceiling hosts three craters that give an impression of erupting volcanoes when lights are on.

Designer: Mariam Ayvazyan
Photographer: Mariam Ayvazyan

Shade Lamp

Masquespacio presents Shade, a lamp composed with different materials, designed for Spanish lighting brand RACO.

After the strategic redesign from RACO's brand, Masquespacio has designed a new lamp that will take part of the new collection from the Barcelona based brand. That way the lamp will be the first official author design that will be launched below the new characteristics from the lighting company. Called Shade the design from Masquespacio in first case seeks its inspiration through the shadows of our lives projected by the Mediterranean light. Above Shade creates a strong contrast between materials that are not usual in the lighting sector, combining raffia, leather, marble and brass, while it shows characteristics from postmodernism. Last, could be highlighted the fact that all the materials are natural, to make them live together through the artisan production from RACO's collections.

Design Studio: Masquespacio
Photography: Luis Beltran

Luma Mobile Phone Night Light

This tiny lampshade will turn any smartphone into a fun and stylish night light. Just cling it onto your phone, launch your flashlight app, and let there be light!

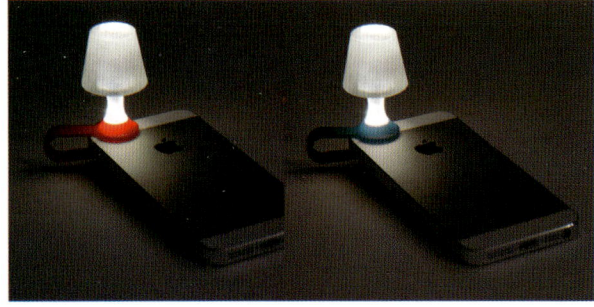

Designer: Peleg Design

Cloud

For the Brussels Design September Festival, Greta Halfin and Kunty Moureau have invited Quentin de Coster to design an installation on the theme of luxury in limited edition.

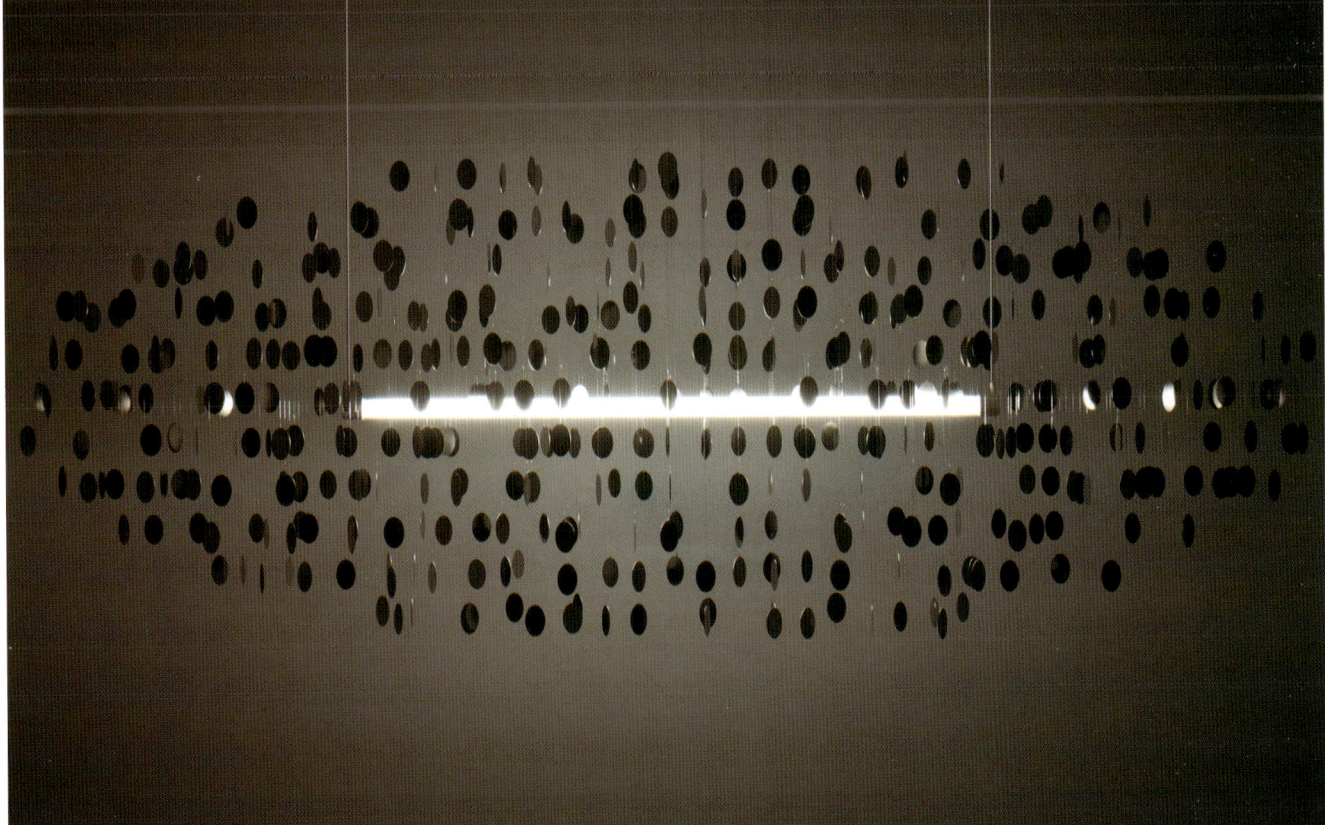

Designer: Quentin de Coster
Photography: Stéphanie Derouaux

Rising Light Fixture

"Rising rays of light…"

To determine the look of the Rising Light Fixture, the core of the Rising principle has been revisited. A design dictates its own form simply by making cuts in a flat surface and allowing it to "rise up". In the case of the Rising Light Fixture, two flat surfaces meet to create a latticework that is sure to catch the eyes, because it gives off the optical illusion of constant, subtle movement.

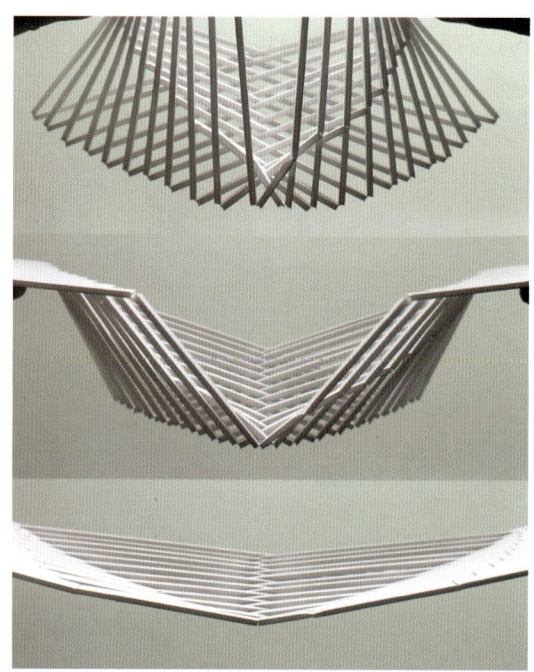

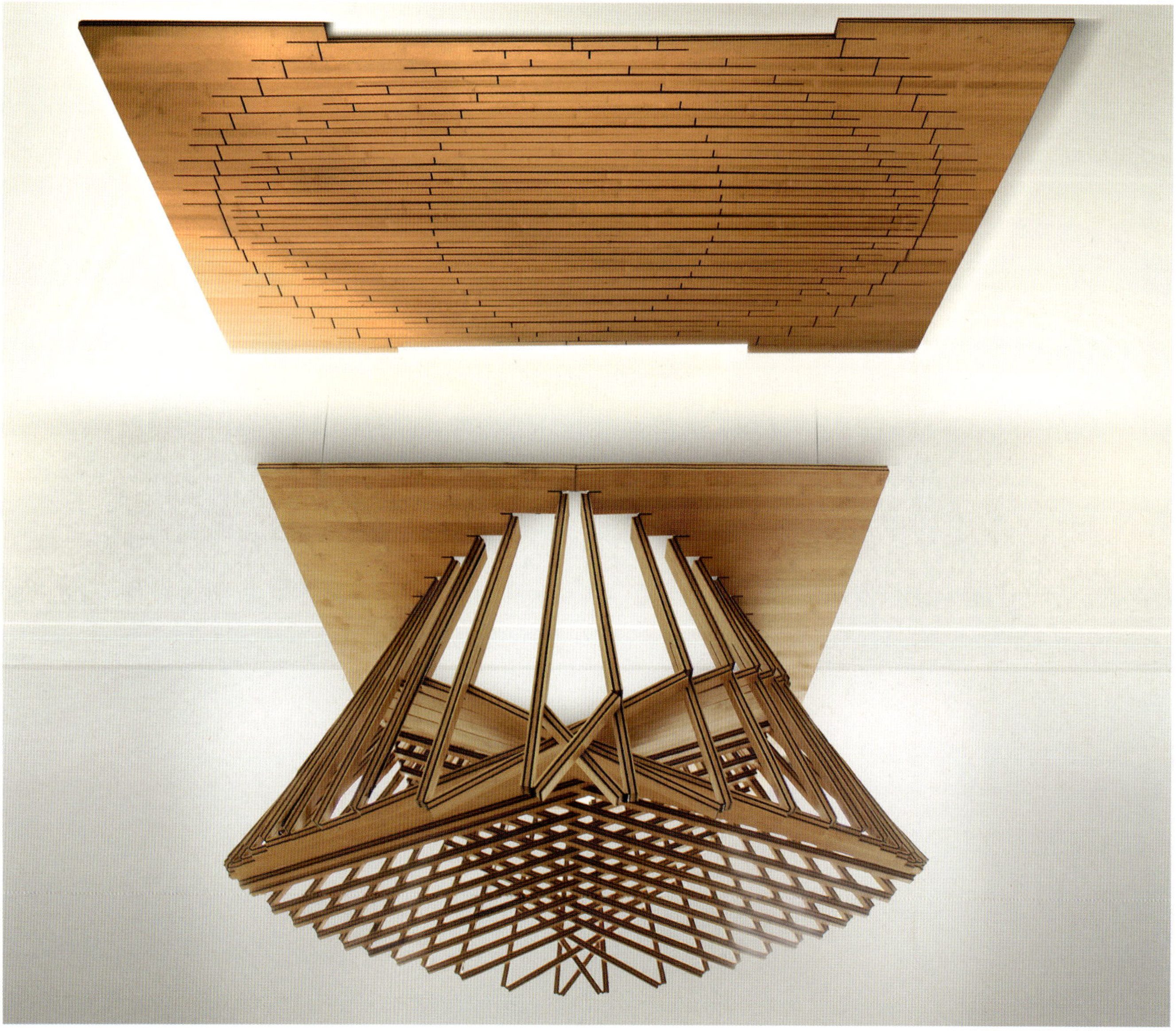

Designer: Robert van Embricqs

Niki Table Lamp

California based Dutch designer Sander Bakker celebrates life with his newest lamp design.

Design can be used to express things that are difficult to capture in words. Following the death of his son, designer Sander Bakker did just that, by channeling his love for him into the creation of the Niki table lamp.

"The project has allowed me to dwell on the few memories I have of Nikolaas, while creating something that he might have loved to gaze at" SB

Designer: Sander Bakker

DROP Pendant

The Drop pendant light features a double curved-surface arrangement which frames the bulb used for illumination. Designed in harmony with Plumen 001 bulbs, Drop features three sets of double-looped surfaces arranged around the center axis.

Drop was unveiled at the 2015 Los Angeles Design Festival. One in a new family of lighting, Drop was inspired by the unique forms of jellyfish. Drop is constructed from laser cut sheets of metalized acrylic with corresponding hardware.

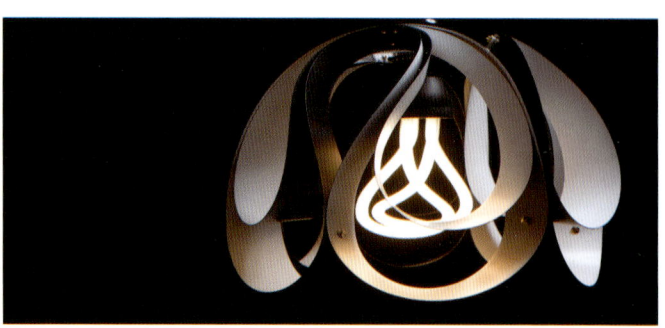

Designer: Stuart Fingerhut
Photography: Ben Gibbs Photography

Nebula Lighting Sculpture

Nebula can trace its beginnings to my enthusiasm for celestial space and interplanetary exploration. From the readings of Frank Herbert and Isaac Asimov to the films of 2001 and Interstellar, what lies beyond our planet has been a continuous source of inspiration for me.

The forms and composition of Nebula reflect an aesthetic not of our present time or mainstream technology — a future scenario fitting our goal of reaching beyond our planet to deepen our understanding of the universe and ourselves. This future scenario frames a vision of what is to come, of places beyond our imagination, and of planes of reality beyond dimensions we can perceive and exert control over.

Nebula was developed during a three-month study period to express fluidity and dynamism in physical forms. Several hundred studies were produced during this process to identify the final piece presented. My aim with Nebula is to leave the viewer with a lasting optimism that there is still more to be explored and learned in our present and our future.

Nebula is hand assembled from laser-cut sheets of metallized acrylic with corresponding brass hardware. Its dimensions are 13" x 22" x 22".

Designer: Stuart Fingerhut
Photography: Paul Vu

Cowbell lamp

Cowbell lamp, designed by Silvia Ceal for the Spanish illumination company Plussmi, is a combination between rustic influences and minimal design.

Design Firm: Silvia Ceñal Design Studio

LEVA

Qualitative craftsmanship in creating and designing objects with pleasure and satisfaction leads to the production of quality items by exploring old and new ways.

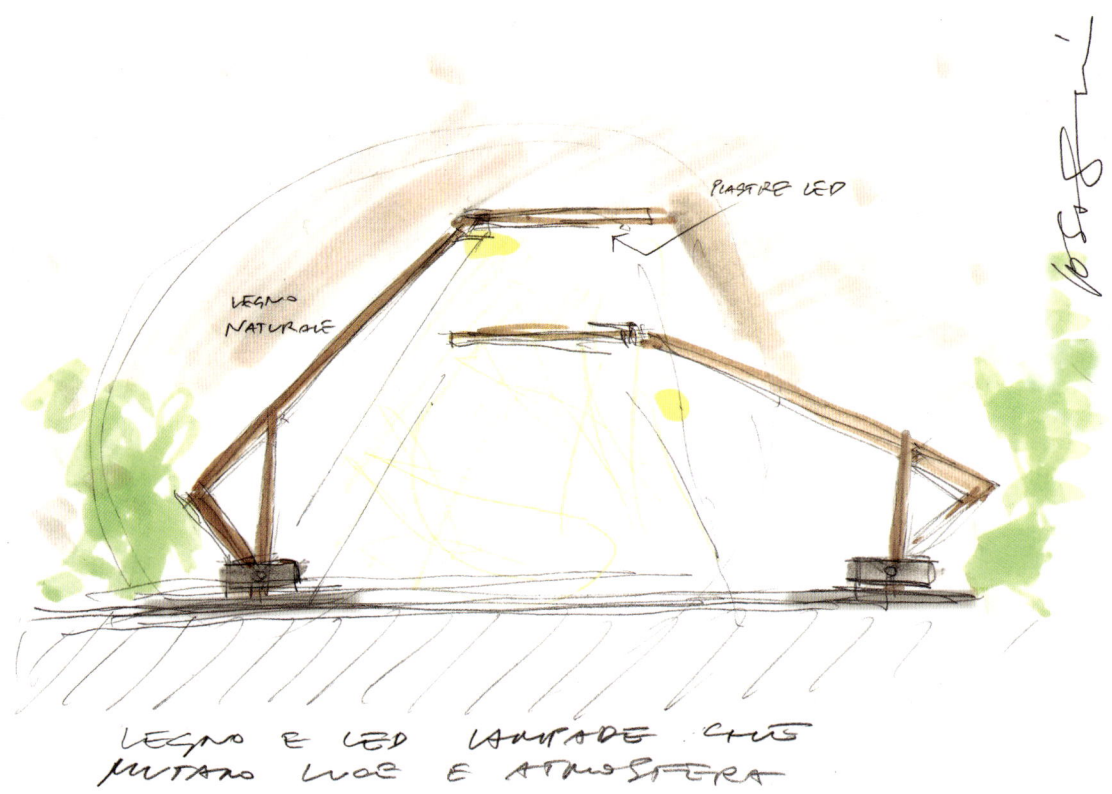

Designer: Massimo Iosa Ghini
Company: Leucos

Bulging 2D and 3D Lamps Collection

Meet ZIGGi, DESKi and CLASSi! The three newest members of our original lighting family. This series, designer Nir Chehanowski, has chosen to rekindle his designs, offering bigger and brighter optical illusion lamps that aim to alter your perception of space and form by using 3D shapes as the basis of his 2D designs.

Our new lamps are inspired by classic and vintage-style desk lamps with a modern twist. In addition to increasing the scale, this series, Nir has opted for an industrious approach to the shape of the lampshade while keeping his signature optical illusion and 3D magic as the focal point of the design.

Design Firm: Studio Cheha

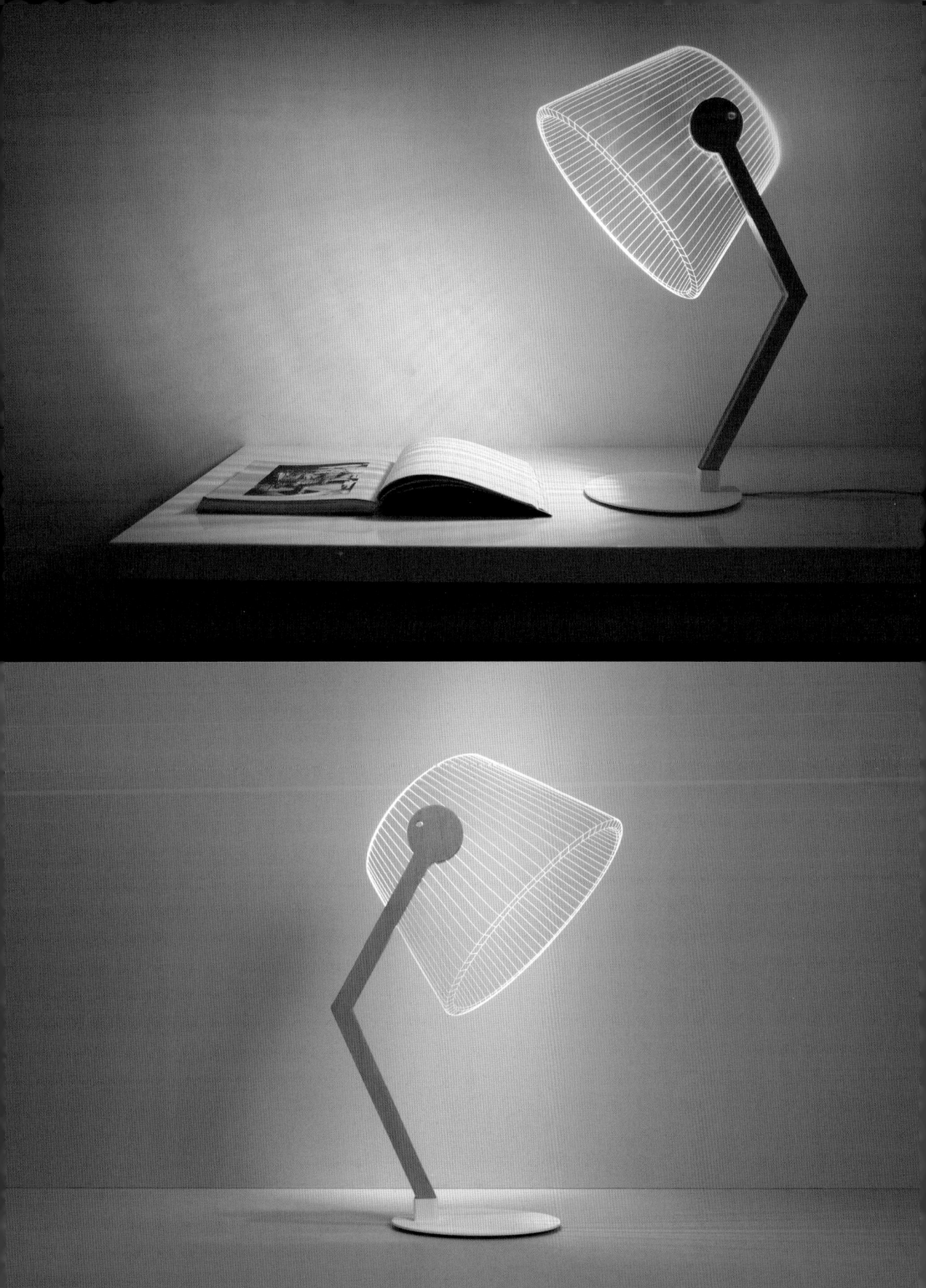

Cabinets & Bookshelves

Grapevine

Grapevine is a wall bookshelf made of solid wood and metal. The shelves, a mere metal profile, are the main feature of this light and adaptable bookcase. Thanks to the grooves on the back side, shelves can be moved horizontally or vertically; they can also be combined with wooden or metal boards for books. Grapevine units can be assembled in series in order to cover large walls with a unique shelves system.

Design Studio: 4P1B Desifgn Studio and Antonio de Marco
Material: Solid wood and painted metal

Client: Edizione Limitata

Mizu

Mizu is a transformable piece of furniture which gives its user a possibility to co-create and give it an unique, individual touch. Japanese meaning – water, reflects well its character, associated with emotion, adaptability, mistery and magnetism.

Designer: Alicja Prussakowska
Photography: Bartłomiej Senkowski

Springtime

A picnic basket, table and chairs, and a cycle carrier – Springtime combines three products in one handsome package. The sleek picnic basket turns into a fitted cycle carrier by sliding out the two side compartments and can easily be secured to your bike rack – you're on the move in no time at all. Having arrived at your destination, the Springtime's basic components come apart and fold out into a little dining set for two with comfortable cushions, in only a few swift moves. Unzip the two sides and find your cups, plates and cutlery ready for use.

Design Firm: Bloondesign
Designer: Jeriël Bobbe

Amber – Side Table

Materials

Structure made of polished brass. Table top and drawer made of lacquered wood. Drawer knob made of polished brass.

Clean and Care

Clean carefully with a soft and dry cloth. The wood should not be subject to excessive humidity, heat or direct sun light. The metal can be cleaned with moist cloth. Wax, oil and etc, should not be used.

Customization

This product can be tailored to meet the specific needs of individual projects of any size.

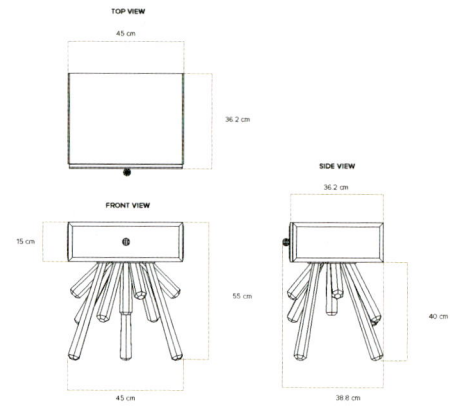

Design Studio: Bitangra

Metamorphosis Sideboard

Arts and Techniques: Wood carving, hammering, foundry, metal treatment, lacquering, varnishing and polishing.

A new take on one of Boca do Lobo's most iconic pieces, the Diamond undergoes a process of Metamorphosis and enters a new aesthetic realm. The merging of metamorphosis as an evolutionary process, commonly associated with insects, with the philosophical connotation of the word that originates from Kafka's prime work, the Diamond Metamorphosis Sideboard questions the meaning of beauty and seeks to provoke a reaction.

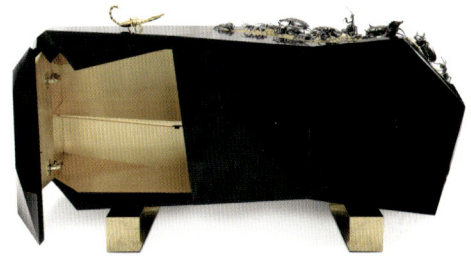

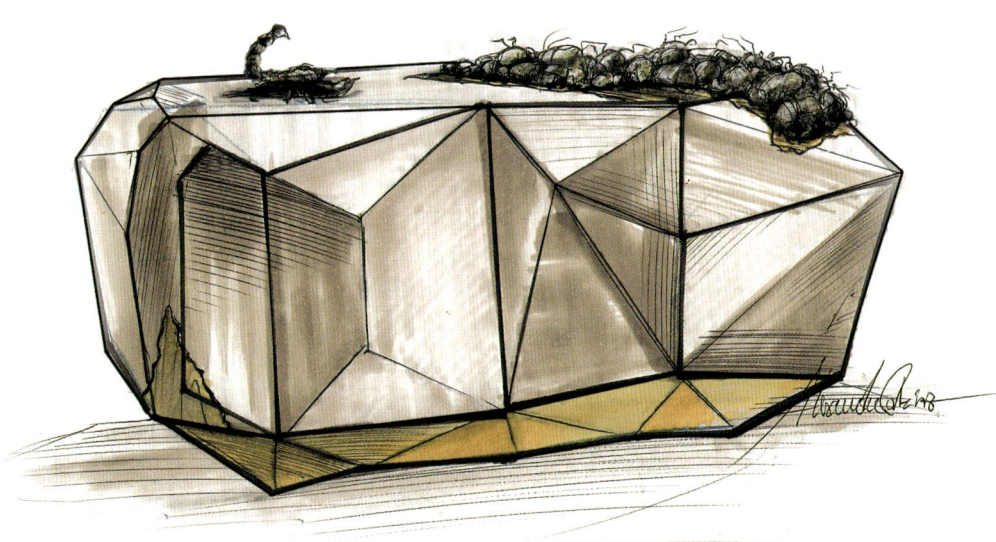

Design Studio: Boca do Lobo

Pixel Cabinet

Arts and Techniques: Joinery, Upholstery, Jewellery, Silvering, Varnishing, and Application of Silver and Gold Leaf.

Pixel is an effort to honor the union between design and craftsmanship. The 1088 triangles that complete this piece carry the dedication and art of those who built it – with a diversity of finishes never seen before. The polished brass base gives Pixel a unique personality, a strong and at the same time sophisticated character.

Design Studio: Boca do Lobo

Stacked

Stacked is a connection system where liquid concrete elements connect to each other while drying. It creates a free way of building, through stacking open concrete molds on top of each other. This technique could be used to build solid furniture pieces as well as complete spaces. The first piece is an abstract shelf where the concrete is connecting different aluminium sheets that work as shelving.

Designer: Bram Vanderbeke

Reinforcements

A collection of structures inspired by concrete reinforcements. Can be seen as abstract building elements to create spaces within the space.

A concrete weight inside the elements is working as a damper to give a balance to the visual light steel structures.

"The Block", "The Beam", and "The Column" can be used as abstract furniture pieces for small storage, sitting, or as a supporting base.

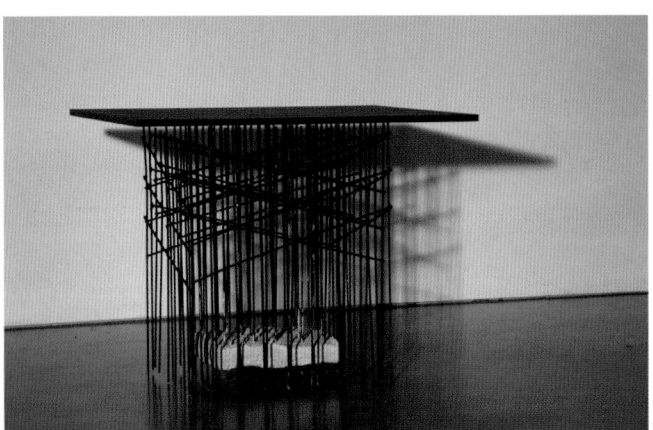

Designer: Bram Vanderbeke

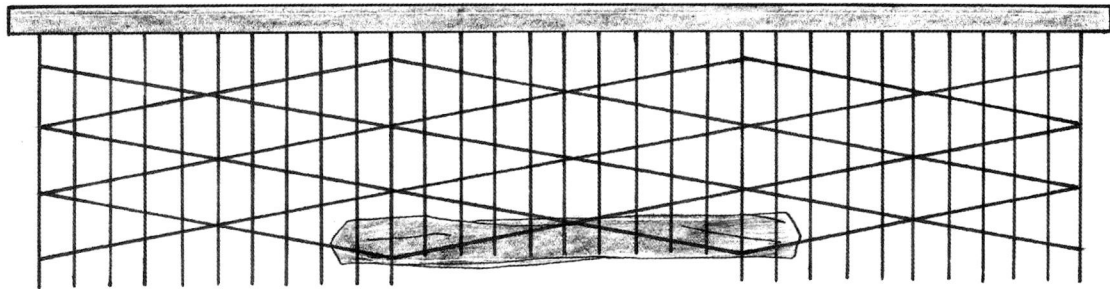

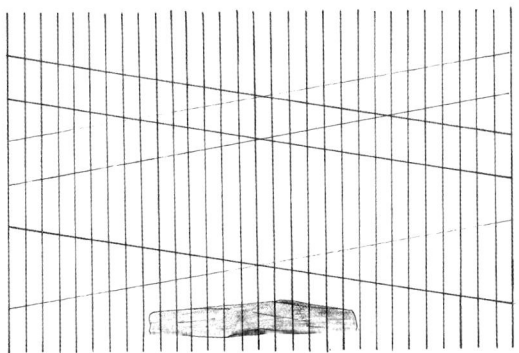
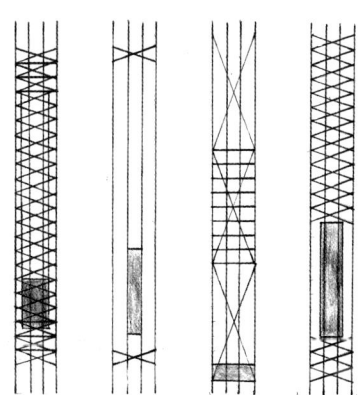

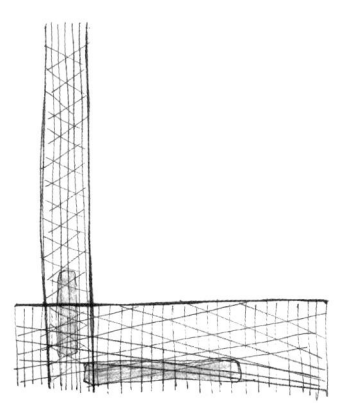

Shelf

Shelf is a chair, but also a bookcase. Comfortable and welcoming, it invites you to relax surrounding yourself by your beloved objects.

Designer: YOY Naoki Ono+Yuuki Yamamoto for Campeggi Srl
Photography: Ezio Prandini

Molly for MEETEE

The 'Molly' shelf series has an unusual expression stemming from the contrast between crisp, right-angled wood joints of the structure and generous, fabric-covered surfaces. The shelf is accessible from many different directions, and has size and presence enough to work well as a room divider. When the doors are opened, the legs of shelf are obscured from view, giving the shelf the appearance of floating just above the floor.

Designer: Jin Kuramoto
Photography: Takumi Ota

Liz for MEETEE

"Liz" is a family of side tables that are configured by the thickness of wooden plywood which is only 6mm. The discovery of the structural strength, new findings of the many approaches and function has produced a new tool with shape that provides number of applications. With "Liz", it is like an experiment, testing the material, structure and function. Instead of a fixed and existing shape, "To be a good presence according to suit the situation" is the purpose of this project.

Designer: Jin Kuramoto
Photography: Masaki Oshima

Palafitt

"Everyone dreams while observing a model, maybe because of the small scale, of the synthesis of the details or because you feel like a "giant", so like a kid in front of a toy.

When I designed Palafitt I 'played' by imagining that a mobile could evoke that feeling but at the same time having a strong sculptural and elegant connotation.

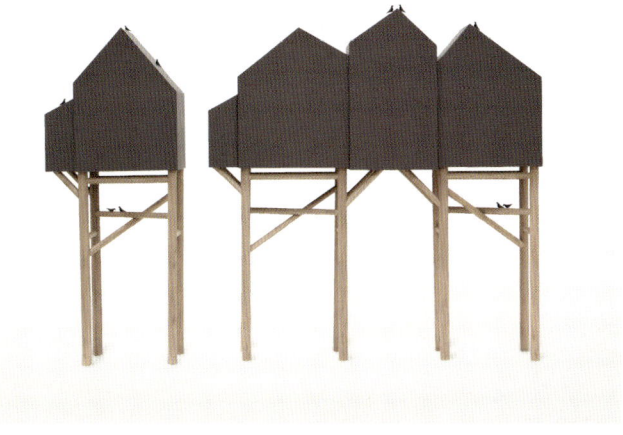

Designer: Marcantonio Raimondi Malerba
Company: Seletti

Tables & Chairs & Sofa

Icenine

Icenine is a wood and brass stool whose shape was created thanks to the expansion of ice within. A geometric solid is filled with water and then frozen until the water solidifies: the volume increases and the box expands, taking always unique shapes. Three solid wood legs support a seat in which the hardness of metal contrasts with the softness of the surfaces.

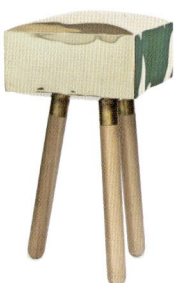

Designer: 4P1B Desifgn Studio and Antonio de Marco
Material: Brass and solid wood

Client: Edizione Limitata

Rhapsody Coffee Tables

Rhapsody coffee tables' family is composed of three metal and terracotta pieces. The shapes of these three different tables are the result of the juxtaposition between the light geometrical frames in painted metal and the rounded thick shelves in terracotta. The slight misalignment between the boards and their structures results in unusual overlaps, making Rhapsody tables dynamic and weightless.

Designer: 4P1B Desifgn Studio and Antonio de Marco
Material: Painted metal and concrete

Client: Edizione Limitata

AtenaSeat and Armchair

The fluid lines take inspiration from the golden ratio, giving the chair and armchair a classic vibe despite their modern design – another way the designer challenges the viewers' expectations. A blend of traditional cabinet-making techniques and state-of-the-art technology, the Atena seating comes with expertly curved wood legs and armrests as well as with a laser-branded leather upholstery which boasts a shaded, 3D effect texture. As a final touch, the blue and red tones add vibrancy to the design, complementing the grain patterns of the solid wood.

Designer: Alessandro Zambelli

Araes Dining Table

"Araes" is an essential dining table, designed by Alessandro Zambelli and manufactured by Adele-C, with folded metal bases, finished with hand brushed gunmetal color, interlocked by means of a central beam, top th. 1.57" with profiled edges at 45° and Canaletto walnut veneer inlay.

Indoor use only.

Designer: Alessandro Zambelli

Concavo Convesso Collection (CHASE tables)

Concavo Convesso Collection composed of table, coffee tables, vases, stools and book shelf, the line is made entirely of marble. The products are a testament of Iosa Ghini's long, accomplished career and the bespoke craftsmanship of guarda marbles & stones–subsidiary of MGM.

Each product is strongly personal with uniqueness acquired through bold shapes and fine-stone color designation. The achievement of each work is in thanks to MGM, whose contemporary production methods can make even the most complex forms look simple. 'Concavo Convesso Collection' is closely tied to the work through which Iosa Ghini has become known, and succeeds once again with elegant ambience and harmony.

Designer: Massimo Iosa Ghini
Company: Guarda Marbles & Stones Srl

Lunapark

This is the inspiration for Lunapark, the new project from Alessandro Zambelli, a limited-edition coffee table created for Rome gallery Secondome. Part of Unplugged – a collection of hand-made furniture pieces whose artisan production is able to bring out unexpected characteristics in the materials they are made out of – Lunapark is made from precious Murano glass using a special technique whereby plates of glass are melted and shaped.

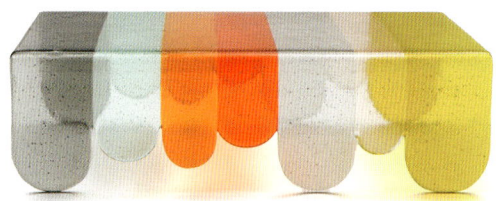
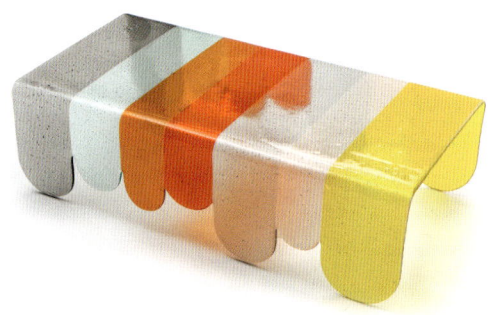

Designer: Alessandro Zambelli

Ori Coffee Table

The project Ori is inspired by the technique of Origami. The idea that led to the creation of the object came from playing around with a paper envelope, initially opened and taken apart, then put back together and given a new shape. The entire structure of the table derives its shape from the artful laser folding of a single 2mm-thick foil sheet. The folds emphasize the 3-dimensional aspects of the shape through the refraction of light that spreads out unevenly over the variously-slanted surfaces, producing light and dark reflections, starting with the initial shade of gunmetal gray or brushed bronze.

Designer: Alessandro Zambelli

Kanban

Designed and produced in Hong Kong by Italian designer Andrea Ponti, Kanban is a side table that pushes the boundaries of form and aesthetic, past and present. The project's aim was to capture Hong Kong in a product: to convey the spirit of this cosmopolitan metropolis at the crossroads between East and West. The concept of table was reinvented starting from the essential components of base and top and an innovative use of materials, shape, color and layout. The use of steel and concrete mirrors the style of Hong Kong's historic industrial buildings–former multi-story factories converted into offices and warehouses. The shape was inspired by the large neon signs that light up the busy streets of Kowloon: the signs jut out into the streets while hanging from a single slender steel bar. The contrasting colors of neutral concrete and charcoal steel give the table a minimalist pictorial quality: they create a chiaroscuro — an effect of contrasting light and shade. The original layout of the flat horizontal top floating above the vertical cylinder base creates an unexpected shift in volumes and an exquisite contrast between density and airiness.

Designer: Andrea Ponti

Clamp Chair

The design of the Clamp Chair was driven by the idea to create comfortable yet light wooden furniture, which emphasize the beauty of wood and modern craftsmanship. Its appearance is characterized through the seamless transitions between all parts. The upholstered seat and backrest are supported by a very slim wooden frame which comes either in ash, oak or walnut wood. The chair is manufactured with a combination of traditional handcraft and sophisticated CNC machinery. Each chair is assembled by hand and the carefully selected wood is finished with 100% natural beeswax oil.

Designer: Andreas Kowalewski

FALDA Tables

Falda is an experiment with slender wire frame metal structures. The airy appearance and continuous lines of the frame elements give the table its delicate character and an expression of movement and balance.The elevated top plate rests almost effortlessly on top of the structural form. The light weight of the table makes it easy to move around and place it where ever you need it in the house.

Designer: Andreas Kowalewski

Streamlined Chair

The Streamlined collection consists of a table lamp and chair. The products feature organic stylistic elements and transparent constructions. All products within the Streamlined collection are composed of individual parts. This results in fragmentend lines, i.e. lines that flow different directions in every part. Streamlined Chair is available in both a transparent and anthracite version. The anthracite version is semi-transparent, so that the line pattern remains visible.

Design Studio: Studio Roex

PIANI Table Range

The Piani table range is a light and minimal design made of two distinct surfaces that elegantly float above each other. The overlapping architecture offers more space to creatively arrange everyday objects. Each element of the table plays an essential role in forming a unified structure, striking a balance between the visual perception of lightness and space. The column design enables the upper surface to extend into the air whilst allowing the lower surface to effortlessly rest between two legs. This lower surface combined with the cross-brace as the central support completes and strengthens the overall structure. The table tops are crafted from solid American walnut wood and the table bases are made from solid ash wood rods stained in black.

Back Me Up

The BACK ME UP is a design that delivers on its promise: supporting you in your day-to-day life. The chair's organic back gives you a friendly welcome and gently springs along with your movements. The high-quality foam of its seat and back provide a surprising amount of comfort, precisely there where it's most needed, without sacrificing clean edges in the upholstery.

This chair's distinguishing feature is its backside. The designer has pulled up the back a few centimetres—a simple adjustment that reveals the seat and allows space for an ingenious interplay of lines. The wooden legs are beautifully received, supporting the graphic design. The interplay of lines is reinforced by the use of matching hues in the upholstery.

Designer: Arian Brekveld

Zoom – In Sofa

The Zoom In is the result of an intense dialogue between designer Arian Brekveld and manufacturer Montis. It is a testimony to the skills of two specialists in their respective areas: the designer and the manufacturer. Both are able to show the their expertise. The designer sees the possibilities and explores their boundaries; pushes, pulls and stretches. The manufacturer, on the other hand, protects his boundaries, name and reputation. And a good manufacturer and commissioner is brave enough to trust his own skills as well as those of the designer. They interact, challenge each other and give each other space, to produce a thing of beauty. The Zoom In is an example of this creative process. We see the functional aspects, like a high back that provides enough comfort, a solid upholstery, flat and sturdy arm rests with enough room for a laptop computer ….

Designer: Arian Brekveld

Amber – Center Table

Inspired by the beauty of amber gemstones, this contemporary handcrafted center table is made of casted brass and marble. The brass legs are produced using old manufacturing techniques that allow us to emulate the final look and touch similar to amber rocks. In the metal legs you can feel the mix of softness and rough texture, result of a very meticulous production. The table top made of polished marble has a cut on the edges that results in a visual illusion of a thin paper.

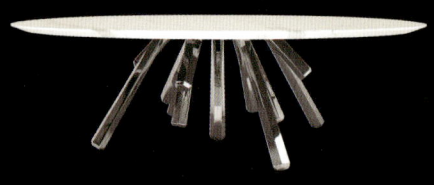
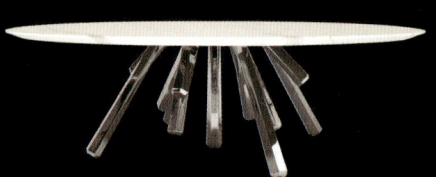

Design Studio: Bitangra

Hurricane – Bar Stool

Hurricane Bar Stool is an ode to the luxury interior design. The gold glamorous legs of this counter stool are made of welded brass tubes, and the comfortable seat is upholstered with velvet. The standard version comes with three footrests, one in the front and one on each side.

TOP VIEW

46 cm

46 cm

SIDE VIEW   **FRONT VIEW**   **SIDE VIEW**

96 cm   75 cm   40 cm

35 cm

46 cm   46 cm   46 cm

BACK VIEW

46 cm

46 cm

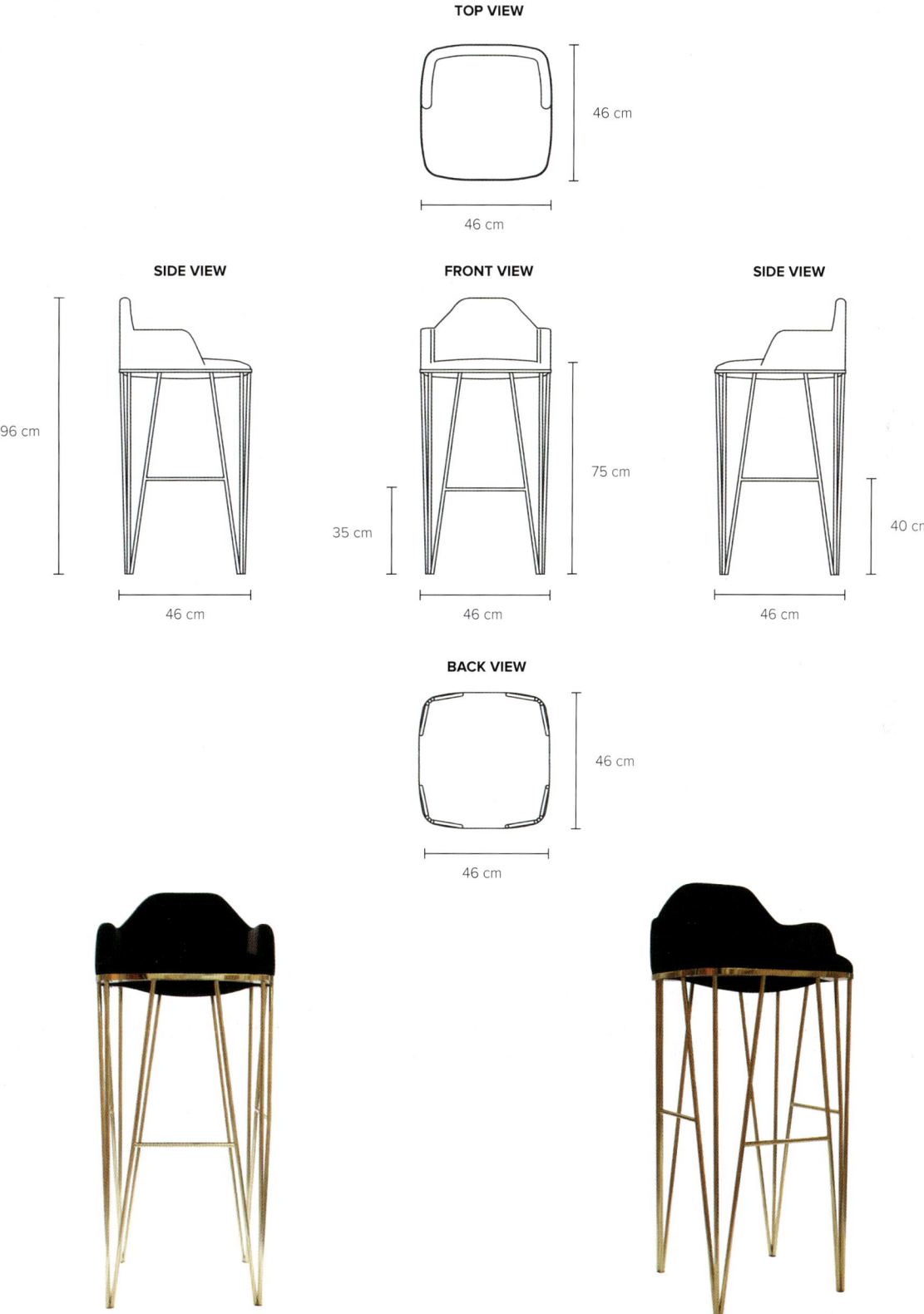

Design Studio: Bitangra

Hurricane – Stool

The gold glamorous legs of this stool are made of polished brass tubes, and the comfortable seat is upholstered with velvet. To give the final touch, the edges of the seat are finished with polished brass.

Design Studio: Bitangra

Nucleous – Side Table

Nucleous is a contemporary side table, with organic form, 100% handmade, made of lacquered fiberglass. This side table is inspired on relationship between the fabrics and the shapes they are applied to. It's like a romance between materials that we have explored, in the search for symmetry, harmony and fluid details. Available in a wide range of colors, this side table can be customized in size, color and material.

Design Studio: Bitangra

Utah Dining Table

Luxury and sophistication are the premises of this dining table for eight. Inspired by the canions of the city of Utah, this dining table is made of lacquered wood polished brass tubes. Available in a wide range of colors, this contemporary dining table can be customized in size, color and material.

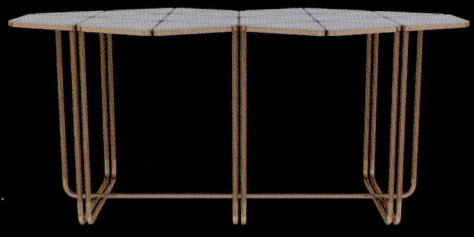

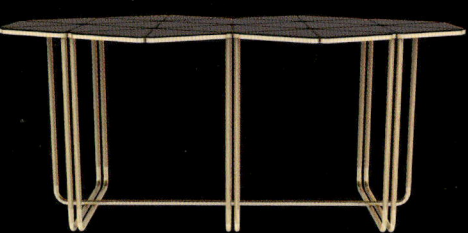

Design Studio: Bitangra

Aquarius

Aquarius is a very unique center table. An evocative of a fine jewelry piece, this striking table blends a certain delicacy with its contrasting strong character. Perfect for your contemporary living room, Aquarius will add a touch of elegance to your home decoration. Its tempered smoked glass top rests on a perfectly curved polished stainless steel base.

Design Studio: Boca do Lobo

Empire Center Table

The Empire Center Table is to find itself in the very heart of the most memorable of events and celebrations. It begs meaningful conversation and years of toasts, symbolizing the union of friendship and the celebration of life. Designed and built to make an impression and deliver an unmatched experience, this exquisite piece will add a breathtaking touch of elegance and glamour to your luxury living room.

Design Studio: Boca do Lobo

ABC

A for accommodating ... B for beautiful ... C for comfortable ... just like every living room should be.

With simple gestures it transforms into a single, double or even twin bed.

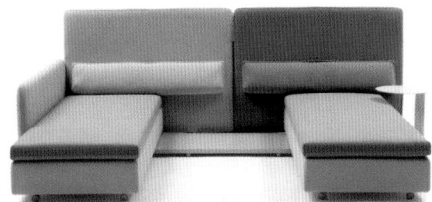 

Designer: Giulio Manzoni for Campeggi Srl
Photography: Ezio Prandini

Gilbert & George

Gilbert & George is a big pouf composed of two elements perfectly fitting together, drawing a line that suggests different uses.

If necessary, the ottoman turns into a couple of independent seats or even rocking chairs.

Not identical but symmetrical... just like Gilbert & George.

Designer: Denis Santachiara for Campeggi Srl
Photography: Ezio Prandini

Nessy

A surprising and flexible sofa, with a strong visual impact, which brings the space to life as a fantastic creature.

The soft and sinuous shape, invites you to a free and creative fruition.

Designer: Emanuele Magini for Campeggi Srl

Ostenda

A careful research on folding, removable and transportable furniture, provided Vico Magistretti with the elements to design this "object of desire" called Ostenda. This armchair becomes a chaise longue with a simple gesture and can be easily moved on wheels.

Designer: Vico Magistretti for Campeggi Srl
Photography: Ezio Prandini

Self – made Seat

Self-made born to prevent the sofa from monopolizing the living space of our habitat. Rediscovering a typology presented in 1998, the seat transforms, belonging to the number of people and the day-times, inviting to modulate space as needed; adapting more and more to our tastes and our desires.

Designer: Matali Crasset for Campeggi Srl
Photography: Ezio Prandini

Beams Chair

EAJY, a premium manufacturer of precision furniture and related housewares, has announced the launch of their first product Beams Chair: Stylish, Ergonomic Design for The Most Sophisticated Home or Office Space, and also introduce EAJY brand into the international marketplace.

Design Firm: EAJY

Design Firm: EAJY

MARTINI

Most of the times, when I start the design of a new product I used to make myself simple questions, by putting myself in the place of the user of the product. When I start asking myself what qualities I wish my product have, a list of adjectives that will define the product, come out. In these list takes priority, adaptability, possibility of personalization, comfort and utility. In this specific case, the product must rotate, be stable, tilting, and with adjustable height.

It also must not go out of fashion and be likeable to the greatest number of people.

I started thinking about the classics, some pieces that stand during time, without fanfare, serene, light, friendly ... and in that way, I started studying a wooden frame with possibility to upholster, continuous, surround, and friendly, with fair dimensions using sinuous lines, linked by way of continuous curves.

Designer: Gemma Bernal

SASH

It is a metal frame chair, with upholstered seat and wooden back and arms. This upper piece, as a continue strip (SASH) is the most important part of the chair, the more elaborated and the one that gives it personality.

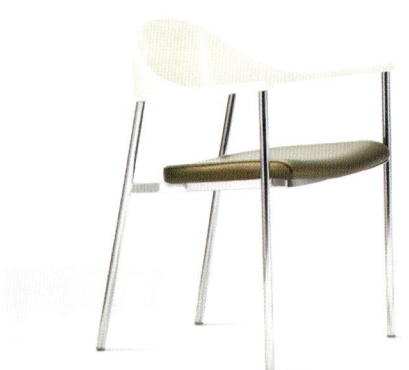

Designer: Gemma Bernal

KSENIA

Family made up of easy chair and chair. The easy chair and the chair have beech-wood structure; the seat-back and the seat are entirely stuffed and covered with fireproof textile or natural and polished textiles like wool and velvet. Thought for contract applications, they find their habitat also in domestic areas thanks to its elegant design and rounded shapes. The chair is available also in total wood version, without stuffed and covered seat and seat-back. There are different wooden colours available: chestnut, walnut, ash grey, semi-transparent white.

Designer: Massimo Iosa Ghini
Company: Livoni

STEALTH Chair

A comfortable, stackable chair, with remarkable features such as practicality and strength. The blunt edges' treatment features the whole product's shape. Another remarkable detail is the leg section's design, tapered for an easy stackability.

Designer: Massimo Iosa Ghini
Company: Livoni

STEALTH Stool

STEALTH is a stool with a strong personality, it stands out for its functional characteristics: entirely made with high regeneration beech-wood, it has a basic shape with rounded corners and flared legs.

Designer: Massimo Iosa Ghini
Company: Livoni

Mannequin Collection

The inspiration for the Mannequin chair comes from our interest in patterns & structures and the concept of changing the appearance of a chair by dressing it in different 'clothes'.

Designers: WertelOberfell
Producer & photography: Iker

Cup Table

In blown glass, it's a small table with a moderate design, small dimensions and precious look. The 8 mm thickness and the rounded edges give Cup Table a particular strength. It can be turned over and become a container or a vase. A simple and creative solution to furnish every corner of the home with a touch of colours.

Designer: Ichiro Iwasaki

Mia for MEETEE

"Mia" is a stacking chair specially designed with compact protruding arm features.

The wooden frame combined with two pieces of planned plywood produces a standard appearance. It is designed to match easily with other products and also suitable for almost every environment when this chair is placed. Stacking could be possible up to maximum of four legs. Storing could also be done by hanging the arms on the table top.

Designer: Jin Kuramoto
photography: Masaki Oshima

Nadia for MEETEE

The heritage of many of the woodworking techniques used by Japanese carpenters originates from Japanese shipwrights.

Inherent in its position as an island nation, it is unsurprising that the maritime industry has been a driving force behind the innovation of wood construction for centuries. The Nadia series has been developed by focusing on a particular method, known as 'kumiki', which uses interlocking construction techniques.

The result is a series of contemporary furniture that harmonizes the design aspects with the high level 'kumiki' structure, as well as giving an affectionate nod towards the wooden vessels of times gone by.

Designer: Jin Kuramoto
Photography: Takumi Ota

Designer: Jin Kuramoto
Photography: Takumi Ota

Sally for MEETEE

With the 'Sally' chair, we have finally succeeded in producing a really strong structure with minimum parts. Once again, we have worked closely with the carpenters at MEETEE in order to find elegant solutions and refined details by applying traditional wood joining techniques of Japanese craftsman. The resulting chair is extremely lightweight and dainty in appearance, with a structure that imbues it with its own, special character.

Designer: Jin Kuramoto
Photography: Masaki Oshima

1141 Table Collection

Kukka Studio founder & creative director, Rona Meyuchas Koblenz, created a limited edition piece. Our founder and creative director, Rona Meyuchas Koblenz, created a limited edition piece, 1141 Table for inclusion within the Green Room at design junction, Salone del Mobile, Milan 2015. The Green Room was a space dedicated to showcasing sustainable design.

1141 was inspired from mining methods in a quarry, the stone results in a chiselled edge.

The designer uses reclaimed Caesarstone® quartz surface 1141 for the table top using CNC machine and then it is polished by hand. The metal legs are hand turned.

Designer: Rona Meyuchas-Koblenz, Kukka Studio

Kettal Bitta

Kettal Bitta is a warm, comfortable collection which features a combination of aluminium frames with braided polyester cords. The new extendable table is available with a teak, marble or aluminium top.

"My aim was to create dense braiding that would still let the air through, reminiscent of the braiding of the ropes used to moor boats (hence the name Bitta, which means "mooring" in Italian), which makes the pieces look lightweight but, at the same time, they look just like cosy nests in natural colours to sit back and relax in".

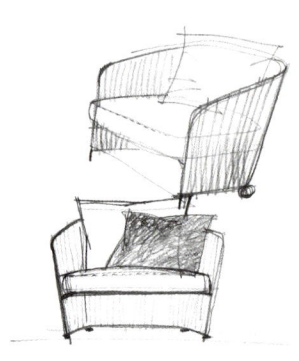

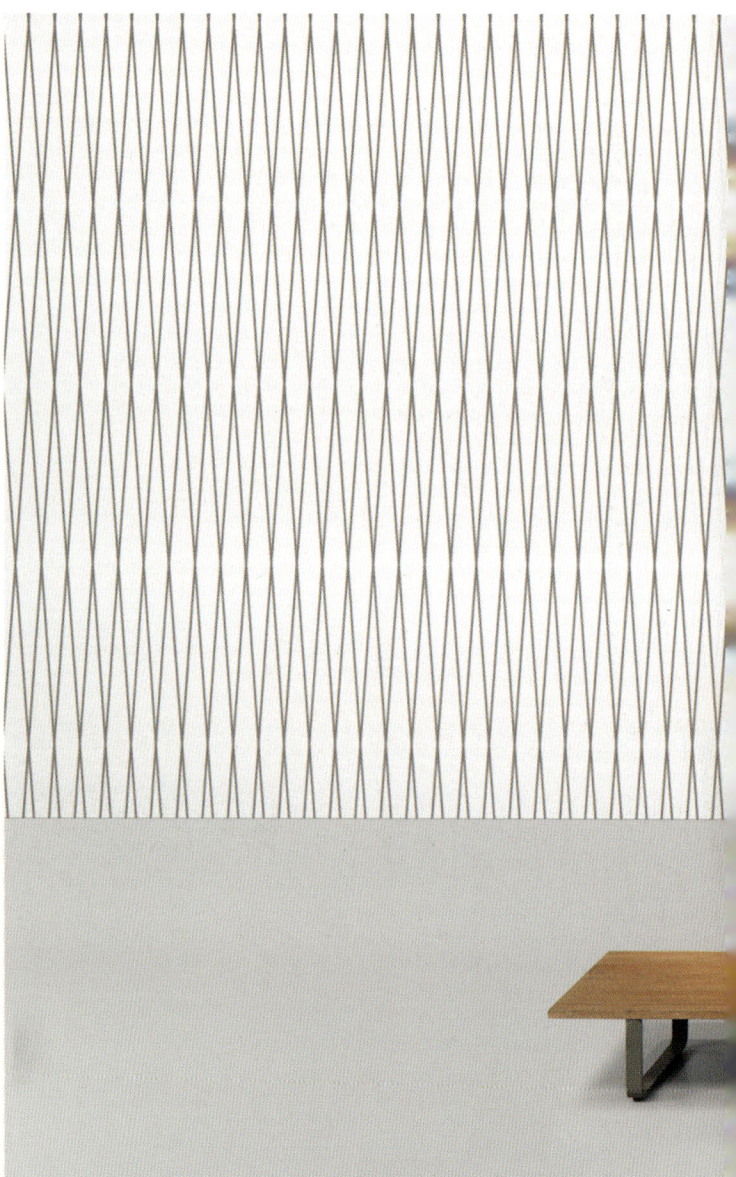

Designer: Rodolfo Dordoni

Antilope

Mario Alessiani presents Antilope designed for the Italian company Offiseria.

Antilope is a flat pack high stool made of a metal structure that support its wooden parts. Every functional part is showed and it is the main sign of its design, highlighted with colors, and becomes at the same time structure and aesthetics of the object.

No glue and no joints, it is mounted just with screws. The result is a solid high stool, easy to mount and easy to deliver.

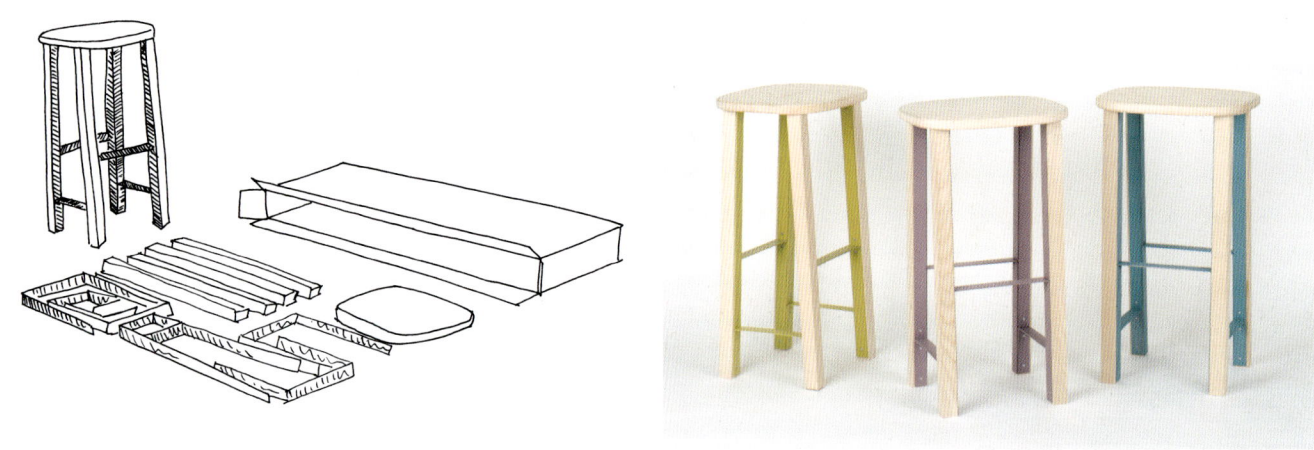

Designer: Mario Alessiani
Photography: Emanuele Chiaverini

Carati

Italian designer Mario Alessiani has created Carati, a collection of side tables inspired by the rings diamond joint system, the setting.

Made of wood and iron, the plane is supported by the metal structure that contains the wood surface like a precious stone. The tables are entirely hand made in Italy.

The main idea was to create an atypical relationship between the legs and the plane of the table, where the structure is supported by an horizontal pressure in stead of a vertical one of common tables.

The result is the junction system that becomes the main protagonist of the sign that is both functional and iconic.

Designer: Mario Alessiani

DoRA collection

DoRA loves comfort in any place. Wool fabric and solid oak legs bring the feelings of the real things. Shape of DoRA armrests and back comes from structure of sail from Asian sailing boat. DoRA is ready to provide you in comfortable journey.

Designer: Miks Petersons
Photography: Didzis Grodzs

Design Agency: NORDI FURNITURE

TiME collection

In fast moving world TiME is one of the most precious things that we have. When designer Miks Petersons run 107 km endurance marathon he had some TiME to think about his life and he understood that in our lives we waste a lot of valuable TiME which could be spend with our loved ones or doing things that we love. So furniture collection TiME is designer's Miks Petersons testimonial to TiME which we still have left and which is already gone. If you look closely from side to the table you can see that it is made in the shape of sand watch and raw oak on top is representing the TiME which is still left.

Designer: Miks Petersons
Photography: Didzis Grodzs
Design Agency: NORDI FURNITURE

DC1 Chair

The DC1 chair is the result of our research, it was created as a support to the Dolmen table.

The intention was to dismantle the concept of shell, in order to achieve a minimalist and living chair black, a reminder of the marble table top.

The matt black lacquered steel chair back, with cold and light appearance, is magnified by a base four feet in ebony, sharpened and reinforced at the ends by a piece of brushed stainless. Steel and wood, that are part of this chair, express both a powerful contrast and a common faceted design.

Design Studio: O Studio

DB1 Coffee Table

DB1 coffee table of our Dolmen collection is composed of a 115X60 cm marble plate, resting on three feet: two feet in brushed stainless and one foot in solid ebony. Everything was done in collaboration with a carpenter, a marble mason and a metalworker.

Nero Marquina polished marble comes from Spain. We take care of selecting the slice and tracing the template with the marble mason, before cutting.

Design Studio: O Studio

DM1 Meridian

The meridian is the result of our research to create harmony, a dialogue with the other creations of the Dolmen collection.

Its shell in matt black steel, its cold appearance and dynamic lines contrast with its comfortable light brown seat fabric, its soft curves and the warmth of its wood legs. The pillows invite the user to snuggle in them and indeed offer him a reassuring cocoon. It was designed for the user's everyday needs and desires.

Design Studio: O Studio

DT1B White Table

Table DT1B of our Dolmen collection is composed of a 210×110 cm marble plate, resting on three feet.

two feet in brushed stainless and one foot in solid ebony. Everything was done in collaboration with a carpenter, a marble mason and a metalworker.

Pele de Tigre polished marble comes from Portugal. We take care of selecting the slice and tracing the template with the marble mason, before cutting. This stone is based on another plate.

Design Studio: O Studio

Brooklyn Desk

The Brooklyn desk provides an urban take on workspace. With its adjustable height and moveable storage boxes, it can be endlessly used and adapted by every member of the family. Slim, rounded legs and removable storage boxes create a simple, chic design. The desk height is adjustable for growing children, up to adult height.

Brand: Oeuf

Slant table

The Slant table was influenced by Scandinavian and Bauhaus design, embracing the idea of straight forward functionalism to create a simple yet elegant design.

The table is constructed of white oak and finished with Danish oil. The table top features a CNC milled surface to create a dished edge profile. Legs are supported by a dowel cross-brace. The overall concept evolved from an exploration of wood plank configurations. In the first step of the design process, an evaluation of proportion and stance of the legs was determined to make sure that the legs were visually appealing at all angles. The design was then refined to add a sense of character. The edges of legs were soften and the table top surface was given curvature and depth.

Designer: Phillip Jividen

Calibre 32

"Calibre 32" is the wheel train transmitting the force of the power source to the escapement; in our case, back in time to the glories of Lebanese civilization, age of the old architecture and the traditional tiles rarely existing nowadays in Beirut, creating an interactive asset for a successful concept where structures, shapes, patterns materials and colors meet.

"Calibre 32" is a circular stool composed of multiple leftovers wooden pieces varying in sizes, accumulated together in order to form the base and the top using vintage joinery in an artisanal marquetry style.

This concentric combination of 32 elements makes an entire entity. The main objective of the concept is to urge our society with its different religions, doctrines, mentalities, communities, etc. to get united; once united, we make the difference keeping the wheel moving straight forward to improve.

Designer: Richard Yasmine
Photography: Mike Malajalian

Glory Holes

"Glory holes" is more than just an ordinary table, well for the first impression "glory holes" is a glamorous object conceived as a piece of jewelry projecting a new dimension in the world of home accessory, it's a multifunctional object the main function of it is a "soliflore groupage" or a group of small vases from which came the word "glory", when gathered on the perforated marble top the whole piece form a low table, a side table as well as a sculptural decorative central piece or when turned upside down it creates a base for a bigger table top…but certainly it's more like a interactive installation, not to mention those who have a playful kinky mind, well a "sex toy" is a part of the concept noting that the multi size phallic rods are easily removable mainly to facilitate the assemblage of the whole piece.

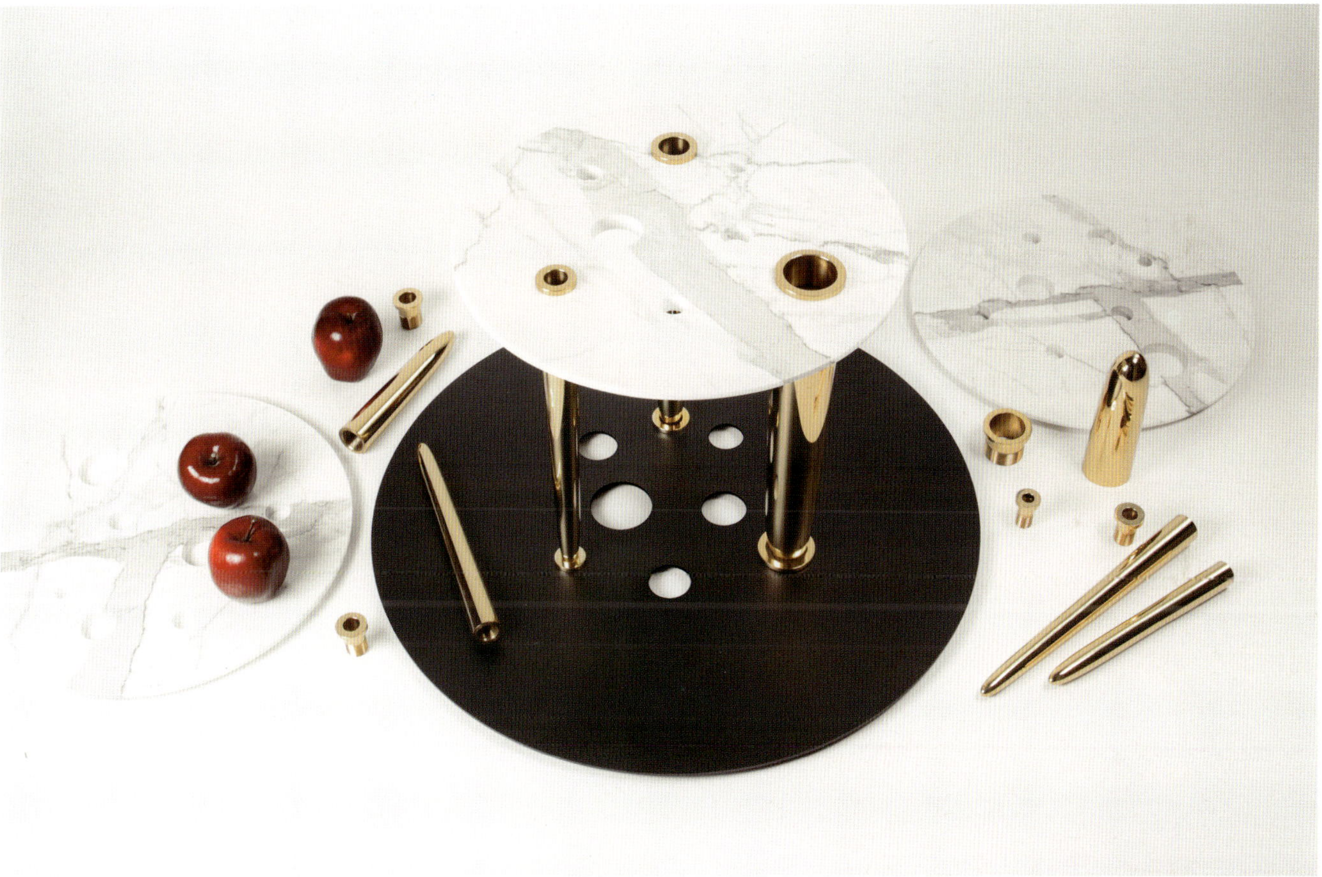

Designer: Richard Yasmine
Photography: Mike Malajalian

Khayzaran / Fairuz

Khayzaran / Fairuz 's main objective is to bring back to life a chair and other home accessories used while sipping coffee, playing card, eating around a table, furniture that witnessed war and peace, funerals and wedding events... Now let's remove the dust, display the whole set fully dressed and let them show off.

Designer: Richard Yasmine
Photography: Bizarre Beirut, Ieva Saudargaite

The Rising Chair

The Rising Chair emphasizes the natural shape an object can made by transforming itself. Every piece of the chair has his own task to succeed in this transformation.

It's very easy to gather a huge collection of different chairs, throughout the years there has been a staggering abundance of them, in all shapes and sizes. But what fascinated me during my research was a simple question: to what degree is the object you're creating capable of dictating its own design? Is it even possible for an object to 'tell' for which form its best suited? And if so, what will the end result be?

Following this train of thought led me to discover several interesting options to create a new kind of chair. The foundation of any chair is the flat surface you'll eventually sit down on. Using this notion as a starting point, I made several cuts in the flat surface and pulled up the different beam-like strands of cut surface. This created the preliminary but already distinct features of any chair: back, seat and legs. The rhythm of the wooden beams gives the chair an organic shape. The cuts are most visible when the chair is still down. But at that stage of the construction, I still didn't know what shape the chair would take in the end. This was determined by the various arches of the wooden beams the chair is made of. Folding the chair into its definitive form, as a creator, a special connection to the material was born.

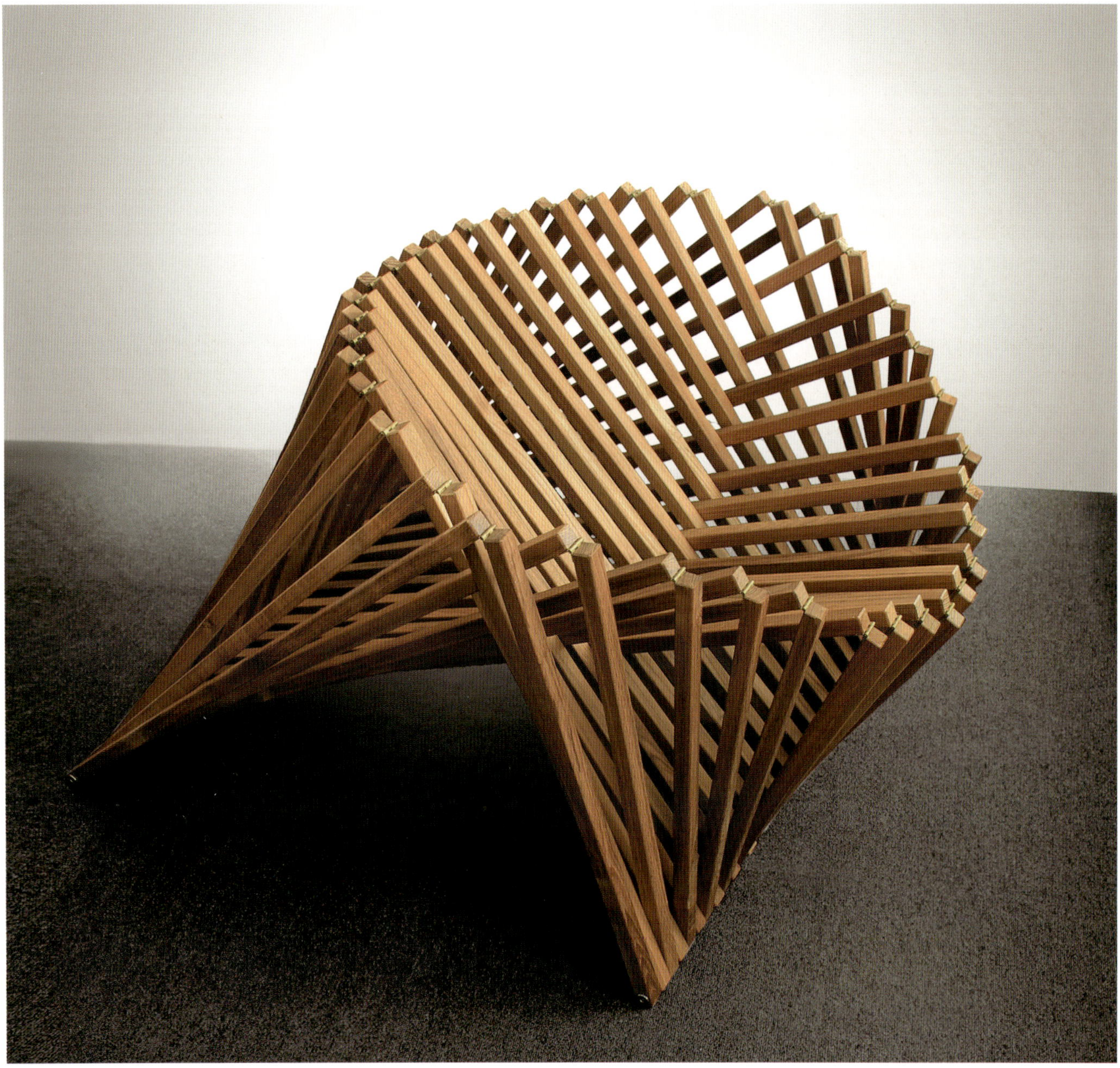

Designer: Robert van Embricqs

Rising Table

The Rising Table concept is part of the Rising furniture formula. This means that once again, the origins of this design can be traced back to the rather simple idea of starting with a flat surface that is capable of transforming into a piece of stylishly designed furniture. In designing the Rising Table, I felt it was of paramount importance that the source materials both dictated and guided the ultimate design, while ensuring practical appliance and usability.

During the design process, I made a point of sticking as close to nature as possible. Using natural design concepts for inspiration, I studied the various ways in which transformations take place in nature without the cumbersome involvement of man. This inspired the incision pattern in the flat surface of the wood that resulted into the creation of a latticework of 'woven' bamboo beams that make up the center of the table.

Designer: Robert van Embricqs

Basoa Table

Inspired by the pine trees found in the vast forests of the French region of Les Landes, the Basoa table is both simple and timeless. What sets it apart from other tables, however, is the original and unique union between the stretcher and the leg. This table is designed by Silvia Ceñal for Treku.

Design Firm: Silvia Ceñal Design Studio

Oma Collection

Oma is distinguished for its minimalist and original design. Timeless and contemporary style, functional and practice family for outdoor and indoor use.

Design Firm: Silvia Ceñal Design Studio

Collection 22

Collection 22 was a fantastic opportunity to create social links and stimulate meetings and exchanges between Saint Denis inhabitants from all walks of life, thanks to local knowledge, an understanding of the communities needs and a promotion of young skilled woodwork students. The collection is intended to further help and encourage these exchanges for generations to come.

Design Firm: Studio Dessuant Bone
Photography: Studio Dessuant Bone

Tubus Beach

Studio Roex toys with the identity of everyday elements and moment of recognition. This is done with the everyday object of a steel tube in the Tubus Collection. At what point is a tube still a tube and when does it become indefinable and no longer recognisable as a tube?

Applying pressure to the familiar elongated shape causes the tube to distort and slowly lose its recognisable cylindrical form. By 'flattening' the tubes, the distortion not only changes their appearance, but also results in flat surfaces. These serve as logical connecting points for the other surfaces (construction) and table top. In spite of the distortion, the tube retains its constructive value and ultimately creates a transparent frame.

Design Studio: Studio Roex

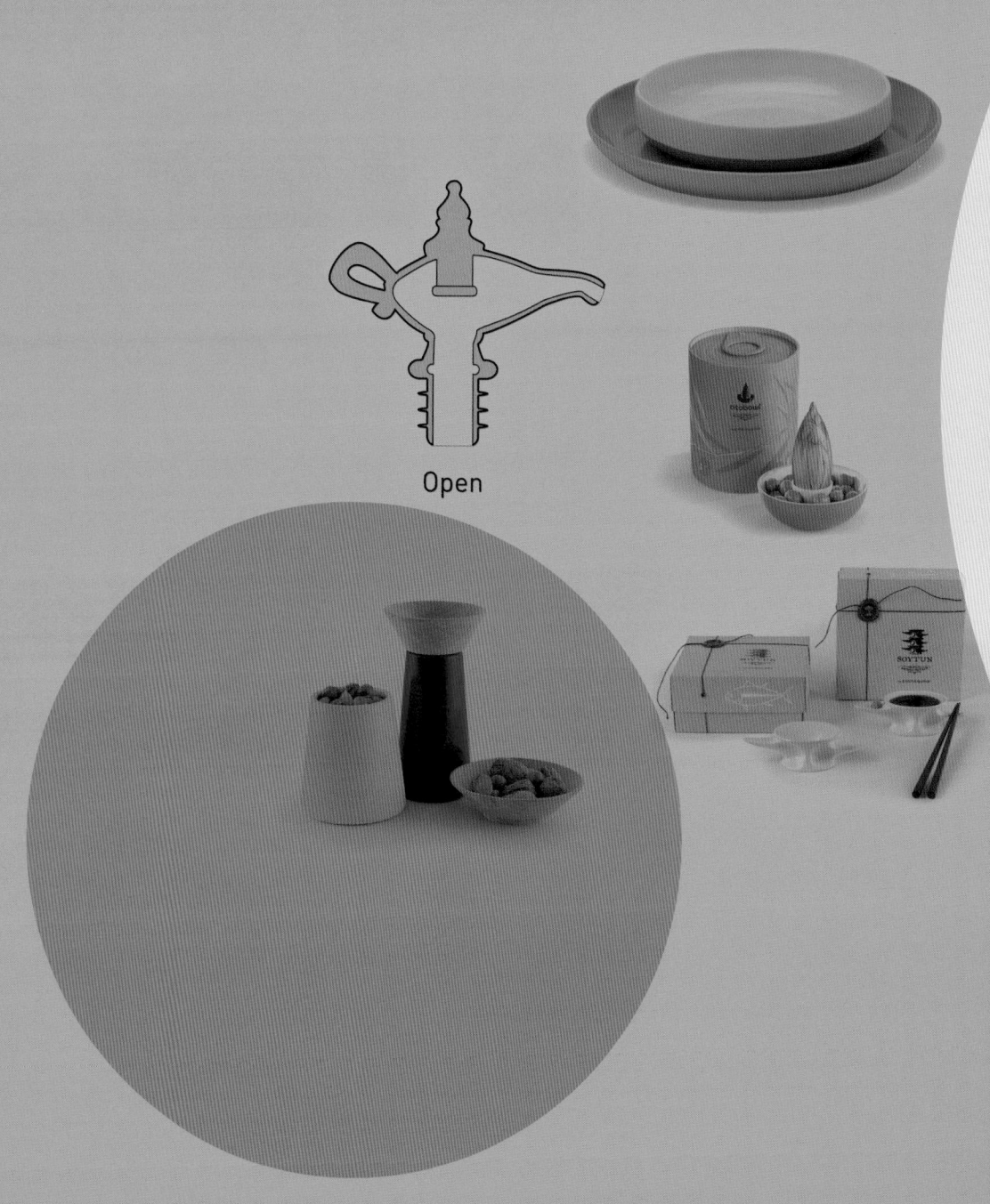

Open

Kitchenware & Containers

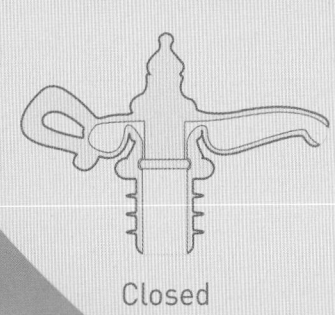
Closed

Batrang Tableware

Like the Bat Trang vases, this tableware is manufactured with the colorized clay and enamel. The combination of the smooth enamel and the untreated ceramics make the series special. Arian: "For the new Bat Trang Tableware, I started the coloring process from scratch. Tableware requires a totaly different approach when it comes to the use of colors." Ultimately, the colors turned out to be much softer. It is easy to combine the separate pieces. The dishes underneath the bowls were given a round ring, to improve the position of the bowls. These rings have been accentuated with a support color, which adds a special handmade detail.

Designer: Arian Brekveld

Blue Collar Ribbowls

Unlike the 'touch of blue' series, which was designed for everyday use, these bowls, in addition to their functional qualities, clearly have a decorative function. As a result, a larger portion of the object was decorated, using traditional motifs from the heydays of the famous Delft blue. Master painter Simon van Oosten painted a customized flower motif especially for this bowl. A flower motif, but with a robust character. This is because the entire motif is painted in a beautiful even and all-covering manner, making she motif almost blend into a full color. In the production of the bowls, the original painting is reproduced through transfers onto the bare shard.

The ribs on the outside give the bowls a masculine air. The powerful lines of the ribs run all the way down to the bottom of the bowl. It seems like they are lifting the bowl, creating the illusion of floating.

Designer: Arian Brekveld

PURE collection for NESPRESSO

A comprehensive series of porcelain cups specifically designed for Swiss coffee expert Nespresso. Inspired by elementary geometry, the circle symbolizes the iconic Nespresso capsule while the square symbolizes the brand's logotype.

The series includes an espresso, lungo and cappuccino cup, as well as a mug. A small detail on the saucer helps the cup and saucer to slot together. The same saucer works for different sizes of cups – the outer rim is unglazed to add nice haptic feature. The inner space of each cup was designed in partnership with the company's sensory expert to maximize the coffee drinking experience.

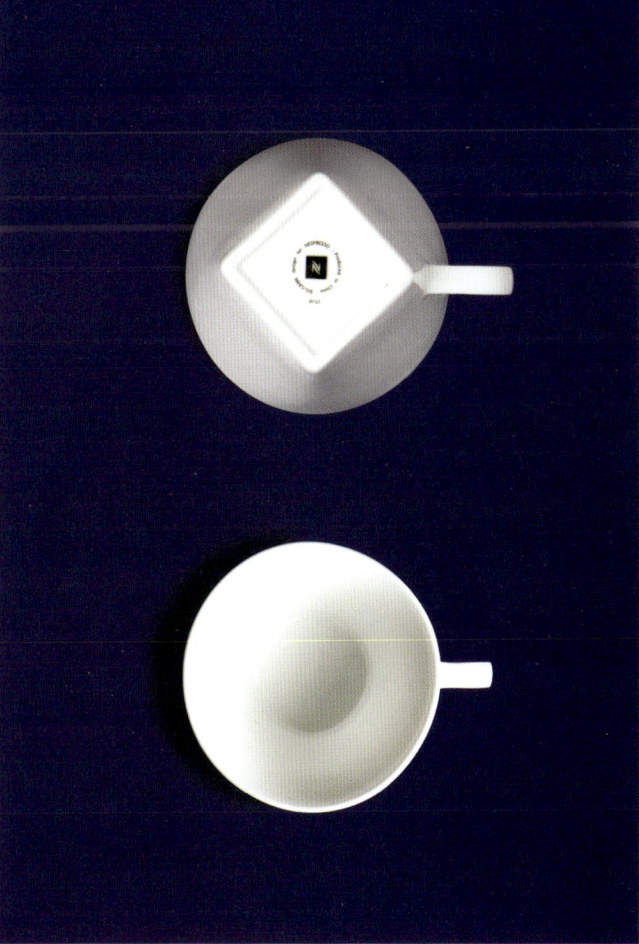

Designer: BIG-GAME

Medusa

Medusa is a fruit bowl inspired by the natural and dynamic shape of the jellyfish (called "medusa" in italian), typical of the seas in many latitudes. Starting from a cylinder of glass, through a long process of heating and forming of the material, the walls fold on themselves. In a not entirely controllable way, because of the different fluidity of the material according to the temperature, some ruffles are naturally created, different for each piece, thus remembering even more the movement of jellyfish, and practically making each fruit bowl a unique piece.

Designer: Giorgio Bonaguro
Photographer: Andrea Basile Studio

SILO

Showing and hiding, displaying and containing: these are the keywords standing for Silo. Four ceramic containers which take their shape from the joint of simple conical volumes that create interesting effects of opposed diagonal lines. Silo has a double identity, underlined by a material and chromatic contrast: the colourful ceramic parts contain and hide, while the natural wood top-trays ask you to lay objects to display them. Silo is an iconic, rational, simple and multifunctional object, perfect to customise every room, in the kitchen as a food container, in the living room as a tray, in the bedroom and in the bathroom as a jewellery box or make-up case.

Designer: Filippo Castellani
Client: INCIPIT LAB

The GOAT Mug

The GOAT Mug discovers how coffee was made and revolutionizes the way coffee will be consumed in the future. Its creator, AnžeMiklavec, decided to create this one-of-a-kind coffee mug that will bring a whole new dimension to coffee drinking. He got inspired by the amusing story of coffee discovery that goes back in 13th century. The story goes about goats, who stumbled upon a bush of berries and went bonkers. Their adventure seeking shepherd then decided to brew the berries and found out that this black elixir comes with energetic power.

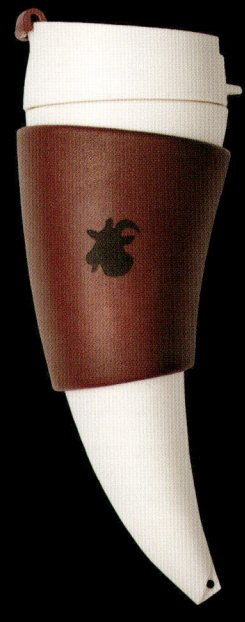
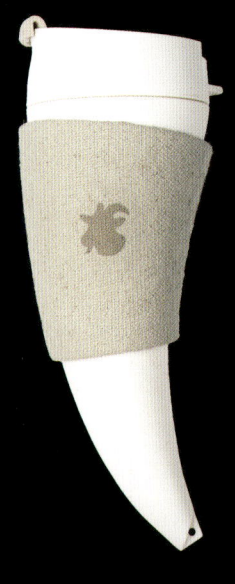
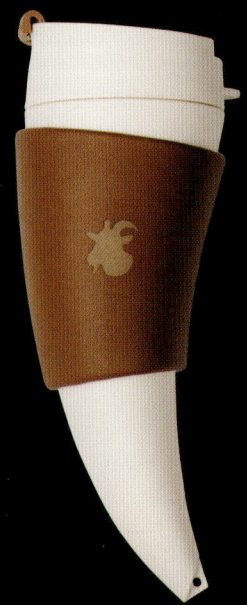
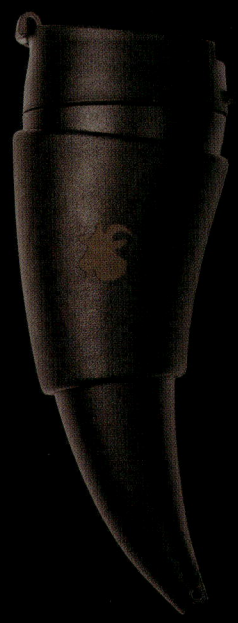

Creator: AnžeMiklavec
Photography: Jaka Birsa

Emma electric kettle

Stelton's award-winning tea and coffee range Emma is now being expanded with an electric kettle in the same design. The Emma kettle is an aesthetically attractive, light blue steel jug with clean lines that matches the rest of the Emma range's blue tone-in-tone shades. The Emma electric kettle is easy to operate. The cordless kettle can hold 1.2 L and is supplied with a removable limescale filter, dry boil safety switch and switches off automatically when the water has boiled. The Emma electric kettle is so attractive you can even put it on the table.

Design Firm: HolmbäckNordentoft

Crockery

This project is the result of a reflection exercise on how to continue working with basic stereotypes that are already functional and obtain contemporary results without formal complications.

The crockery of 31 pieces has been developed in collaboration with the Valencian ceramics company Jose Gimeno that has been developing their craft activity in Manises since 1925.

Design Firm/Designer: Nueve estudio
Photography: David M. Cordón

A Collection of Creative Furniture and Household

Kitchen Herb Pot

Kitchen herb pot: a 3-kitchen herb pot set that perfectly fits in with the rest of the kitchen elements and allows you to grow and have your aromatic plants handy while cooking or directly served on the table.

Design Firm/Designer: Nueve estudio
Photography: David M. Cordón

Babu Toothpick Holder

What a spiritual experience! This meditating guru will sit calmly on his modest chair of toothpicks, keeping them handy and ready for use.

Designer: Yaron Hirsch for Peleg Design

Oiladdin Pourer & Stopper

This legendary oil lamp can grant you three wishes: easily poured olive oil, a clever seal to keep it fresh, and a magical look that adds charm to your bottle!

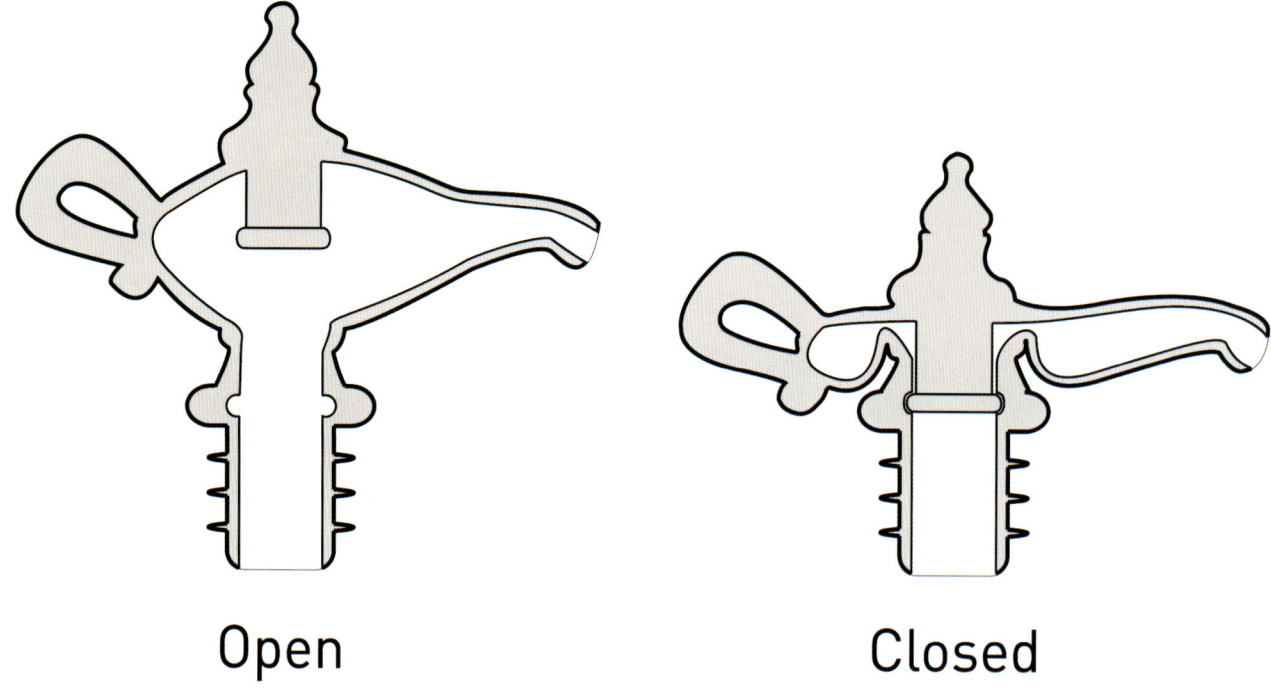

Open　　　　　　　　Closed

Designer: Peleg Design

A Collection of Creative Furniture and Household

Miso Bowls

Miso bowls are highly tactile products in the way they are handled. The rib structure gives a good grip while handling the bowl and insulates the fingers from the heat from the bowl's content. It also hides the dividing line between the bowl and the lid and makes it a uniform object. The miso bowls are made from turned wood, and in various wood types.

Designer: Per Finne
Photography: Per Finne

Naturally Norwegian

Naturally Norwegian™ is a collection of high quality stainless steel flatware, featuring exclusive styles inspired by Norwegian nature. Like the simplicity of the Scandinavian design tradition, this flatware is designed with a delicate balance between form and function. Flatware is a familiar product, in which we relate to with several senses.

The design lies not only in the visual appearance, but very much in its everyday purpose. Consumers tend to hold and use flatware in different ways, and the flatware is given a natural structure to achieve the flexibility of use. As seen in the dynamic landscape of Western Norway, these shapes are balanced between geometrical and organic expressions. The lack of ornamentation makes the flatware easy to keep clean and feels more comfortable in the hand.

Designer: Per Finne
Photography: Oneida

A Collection of Creative Furniture and Household

Ajorí

AJORÍ is a creative solution for organize and store seasonings, spices and various culinary condiments, inspired by the elegant form of the bulb of garlic.This kitchen accessory holds six containers, designed to contain different products used for the seasoning of several dishes, adapting to the different culinary traditions of each country.

AWARDS:

- International Design For All Foundation. Good Practices Awards.

Selected as a Good Practice in "Spaces, products and services already in use" category. Barcelona, SPAIN. 2015.

- A' Design Award and Competition

Golden A' Design Award Winner in Bakeware, Tableware, Drinkware and Cookware Design Category, Milan, ITALY. April, 2014.

- Crafts of Castilla la Mancha Awards

First Price. Winner in the category of design applied to the crafts 2011.

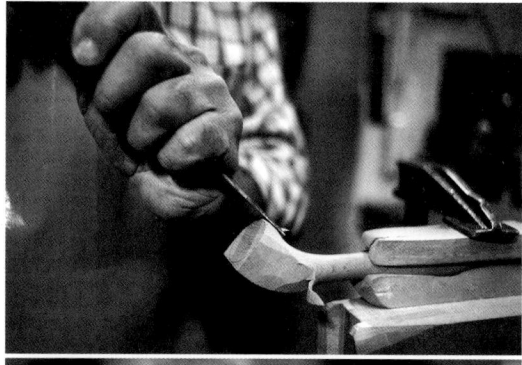

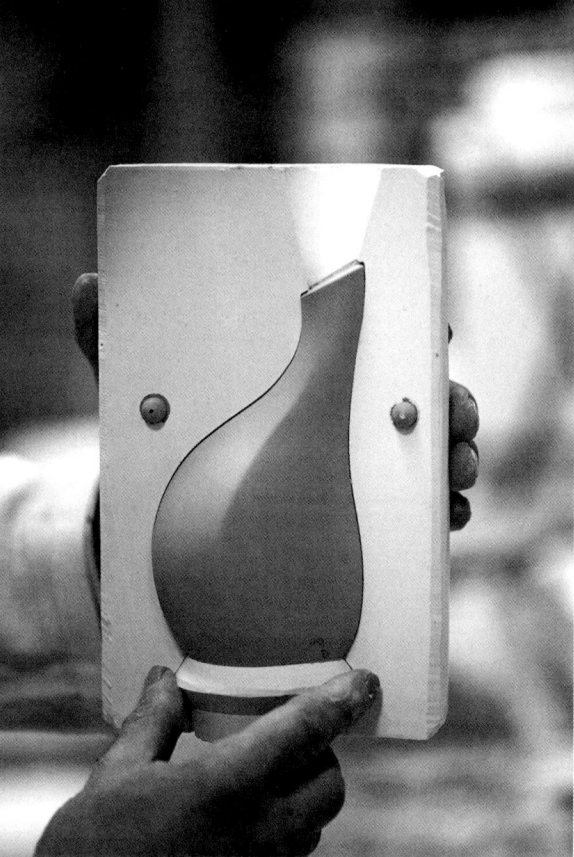

Designer: Pilar Balsalobre & Carlos Jiménez
Photography: Alquimia Design Studio

A Collection of Creative Furniture and Household 169

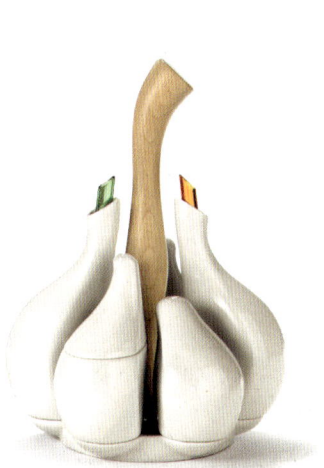
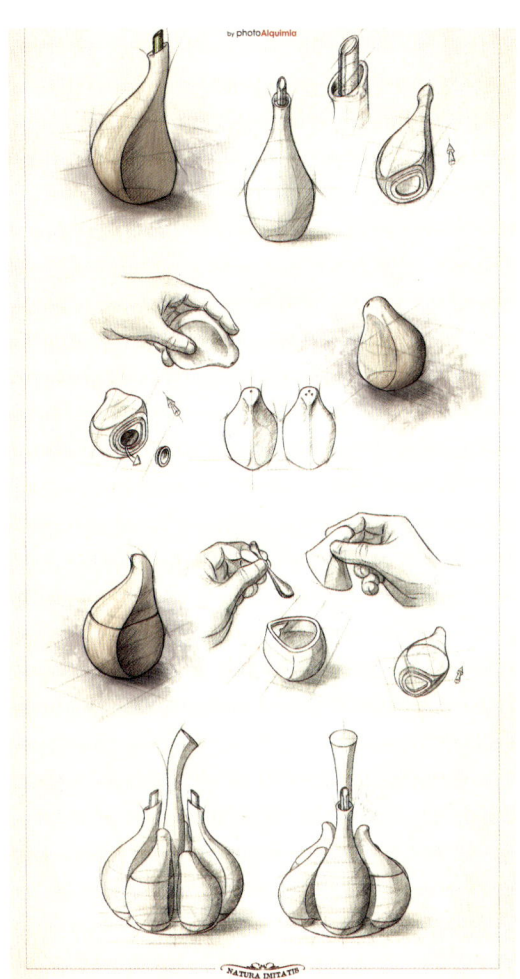

Soytun

SOYTUN is manufactured using enamelled stoneware. Designed for the increasingly common tasting of the various forms of presentation of raw fish such as sashimi, sushi, tartar... etc. This design serves to contain soy sauce, also has a place for spicy mustard (wasabi) and finally has a part to let chopsticks when they are not used.

For its manufacture, we use enamelled stoneware, attached to a painstaking craft production. In the area of the base, each SOYTUN is signed and numbered by hand.

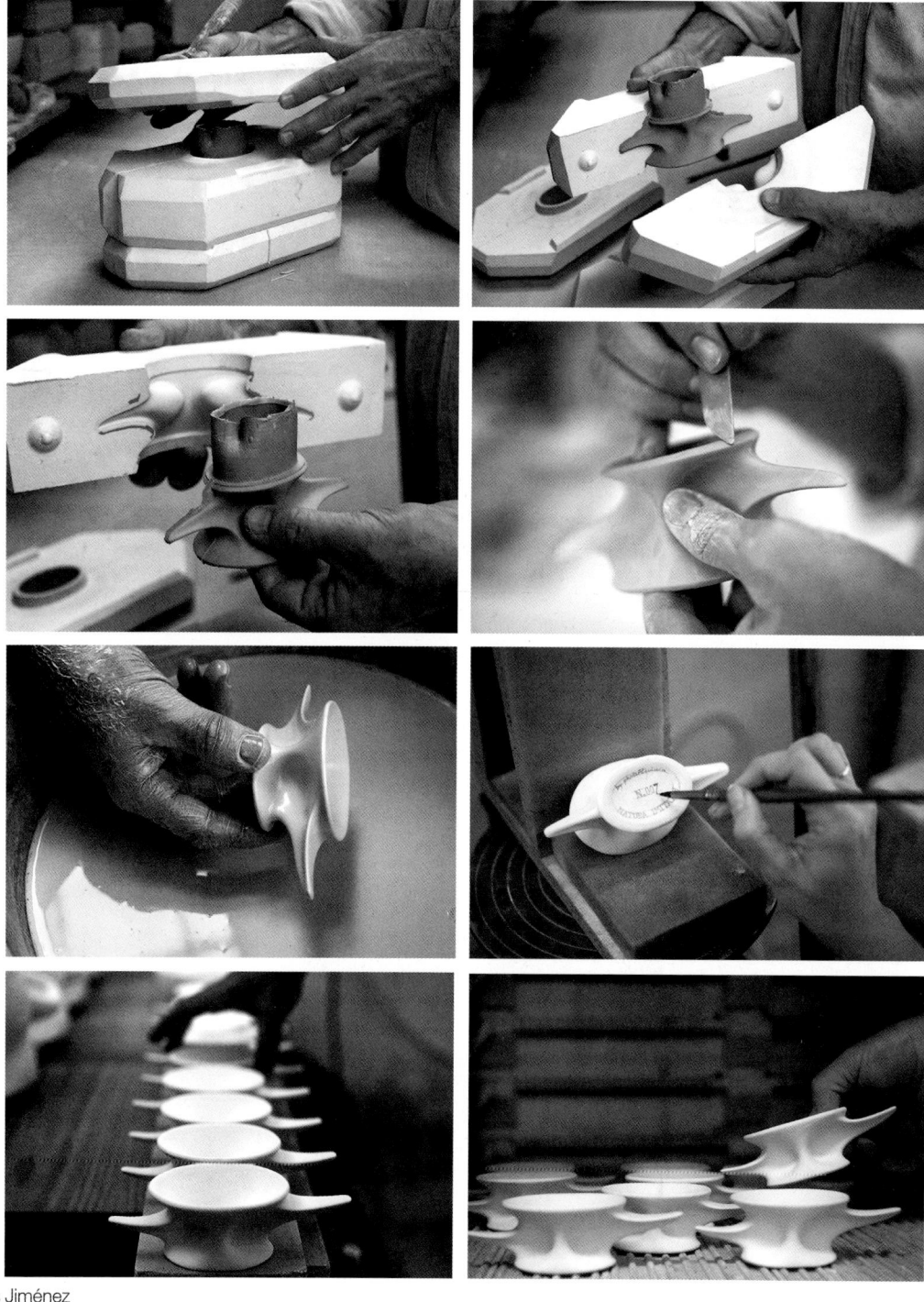

Designer: Pilar Balsalobre & Carlos Jiménez
Photography: Alquimia Design Studio

AWARDS

- International Design For All Foundation Good Practices Awards

Selected as a Good Practice in "Spaces, products and services already in use" category. Barcelona, SPAIN. 2015.

- A'Design Award and Competition.

Bronze A' Design Award Winner in Bakeware, Tableware, Drinkware and Cookware Design Category, 2014 - 2015. Milan, ITALY. April, 2015.

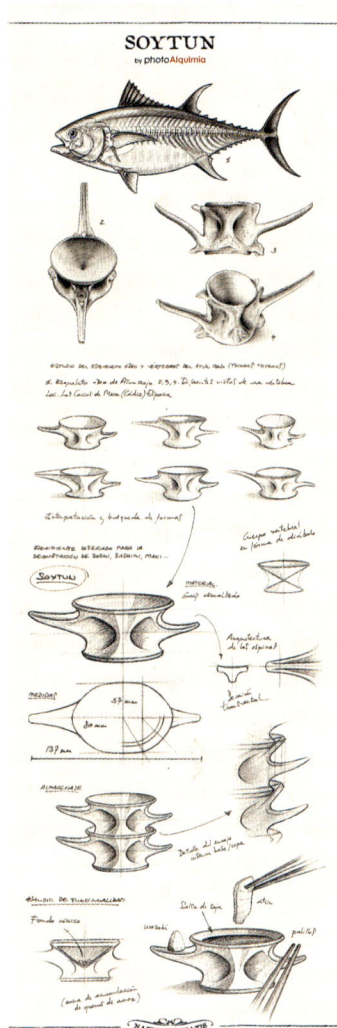

Titobowl

TITOBOWL is manufactured using stoneware. Specially designed for tasting different varieties and dressings olives with pit, although it has been adapted for tasting pitted olives and other snacks because turning the top cap of the container, it becomes a toothpick holder.

For manufacturing it, we use stoneware and olive tree turned wood by hand, a mixture of a cold material with a warm one, attached to a painstaking craft production. Each Titobowl is signed and numbered by hand.

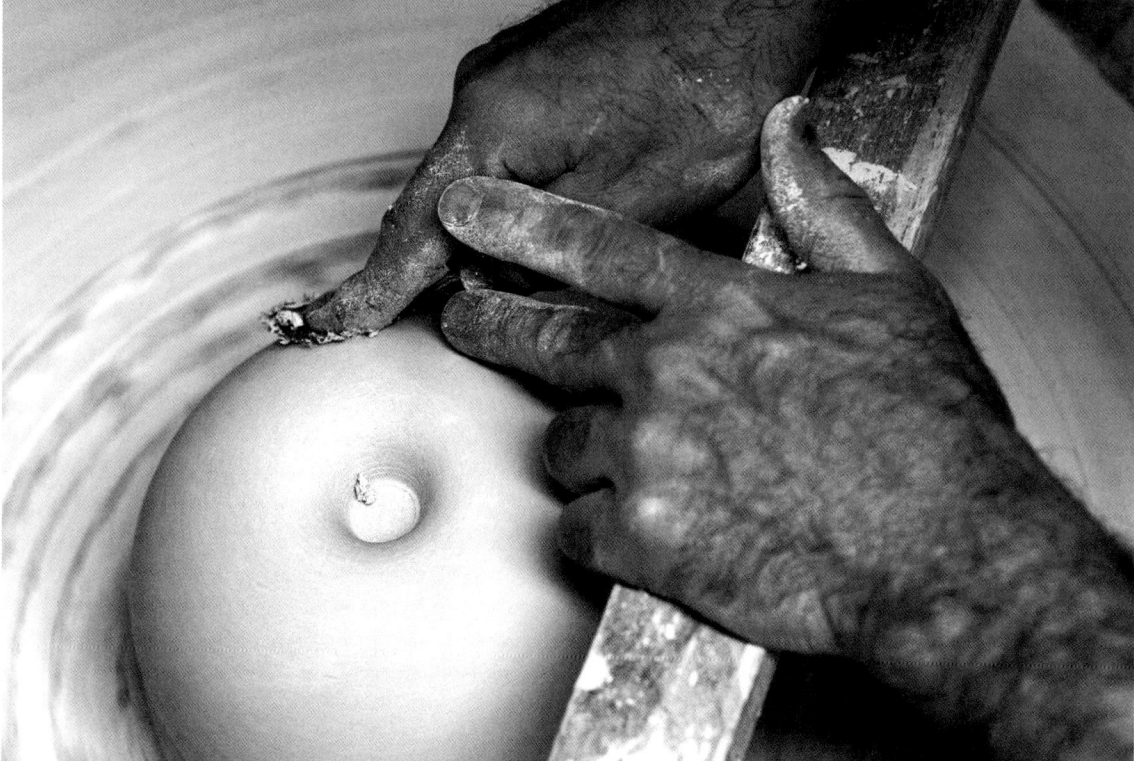

Designers: Pilar Balsalobre & Carlos Jiménez
Photography: Alquimia Design Studio

AWARDS

- International Design For All Foundation Good Practices Awards

Selected as a Good Practice in "Spaces, products and services already in use" category. Barcelona, SPAIN. 2015.

- A'Design Award and Competition.

Golden A' Design Award Winner in Bakeware, Tableware, Drinkware and Cookware Design Category, 2014 - 2015. Milan, ITALY. April, 2015.

Ommo

Diga, Koma and Torus are three kitchen utensils designed for Ommo, a new design-oriented brand introduced at the Ambiente show in February 2016. Minimalist approach, bright colors, stainless steel and matte plastic, abstract shapes and curved lines are the defining features of these products designed to be extremely functional, user-friendly and fun.

Diga and Torus won the Good Design Award 2016

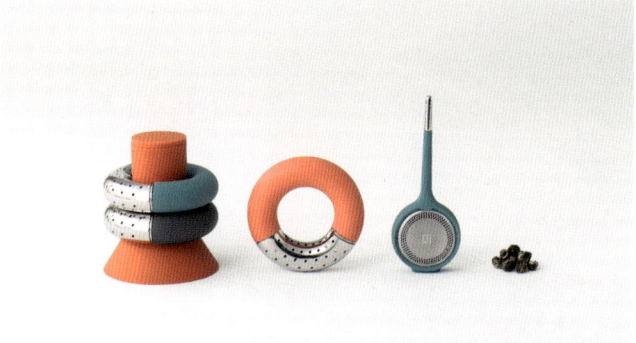
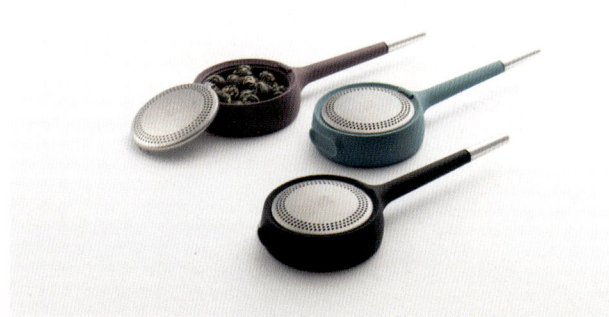

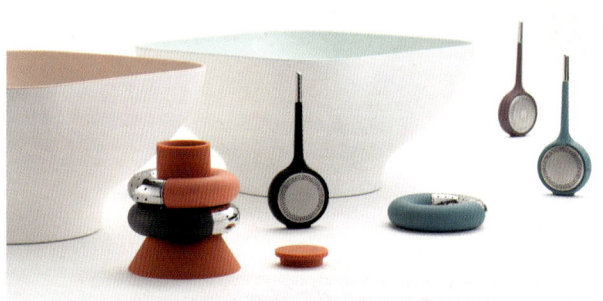

Design Agency: Ponti Design Studio Limited

EM77 Vacuum Jug

The vacuum jug with the unique rocker stopper was created by Erik Magnussen and is one of Stelton's best-selling designs ever. Besides the rocker stopper it has a screw cap for transportation of liquids.

This is the ABS plastics version but it is also available in a stainless steel and a soft coated version. The recent years it has become quite a fashion icon setting the trend every spring and autumn with new seasonal colours.

Awards

Danish Design Award (Classic Category, 2007), iF Design Award, 1992 and ID Prize, 1977.

Design Studio: Erik Magnussen

Emma Mugs

The award-winning Emma collection beautifies everyday life with its attractive designs for the tea and coffee table. The collection is characterised by strong, simple lines and remains focused on the form and function of the design. With its innovative combination of steel, wood and stoneware it is a new design classic for the tea and coffee table. Emma is now available in blue and grey tone-on-tone colours.

Awards

Special mention GDA 2015, iF Product Design Award 2014, Red Dot Design Award 2014

Design: HolmbäckNordentoft

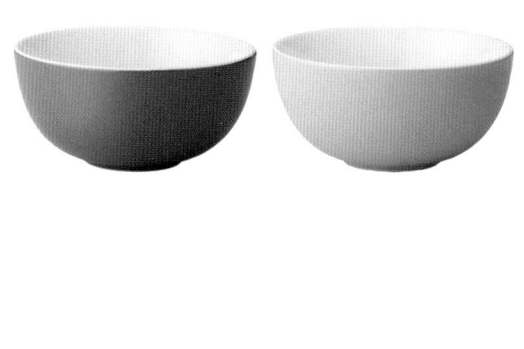

Design: HolmbäckNordentoft

Awaken your curiosity …

Minimalist, elegant and discreet. Hide sweet treats, jewellery or keys in this beautiful bonbonniere designed by the internationally renowned designer Mikaela Dörfel. Peak is an elegant bonbonniere with a brushed brass surface, which will adorn any living room table, bedside table or bookshelf. The design's tight, consistent line is broken by a spontaneous, playful crest on the bonbonniere's lid.

Design: Mikaela Dörfel

The popular, award-winning Theo collection by Francis Cayouette now has a serving tray in stunning bamboo, to complete the entire range. With its aesthetic contrasts, the Theo range has been designed to stimulate the senses. The modern design and sensory material combinations of black stoneware and bamboo have won an international design award—the impressive IF design award 2015. Complete the look of your set with this new tray.

Design: Francis Cayouette

no side is the wrong side.
Enjoy hot or cold drinks without spilling when you are on the move. It's smart, stylish design and functionality in a cup—choose your favorite version in colored ABS plastic or steel. All cups are BPA and phthalate free. Now it is even easier to take your favorite beverage with you.

Design: Stelton

MatreshKit — Four-Item Kitchenware Set

Each doll can be made in individual colour and material. There are options of matt plastic, metal and wood. It is possible to apply an original glossy floral pattern on plastic and metal dolls. The mechanism of doll-mills is specifically designed for ease of use. It is simple to put together and take apart, and it is protected against spilling excess grind inside the structure, regardless of chosen material (each material has its own optimal technological implementation).

Russian doll's shape designed to fit perfectly in the hand without slipping out of it.

There is a possibility to mark pepper and salt by engraving.

A Russian doll set will decorate the interior of any style, whether it is a Provençal kitchen or a high-tech one.

Thickened bottom for stability

MatreshKit includes

—a pepper mill h = 14 cm
—a salt mill, 12 cm
—a case for toothpicks, 9 cm
—a kitchen timer, 6 cm

5-minute timer

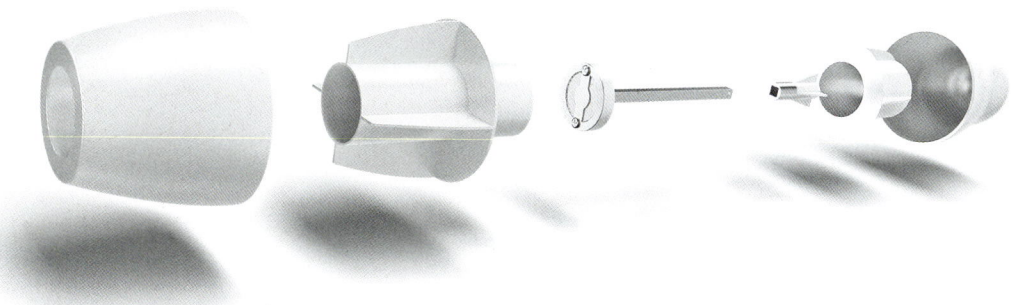

Design Firm: Const Lab
Art-director: Vitaly Konstantinov

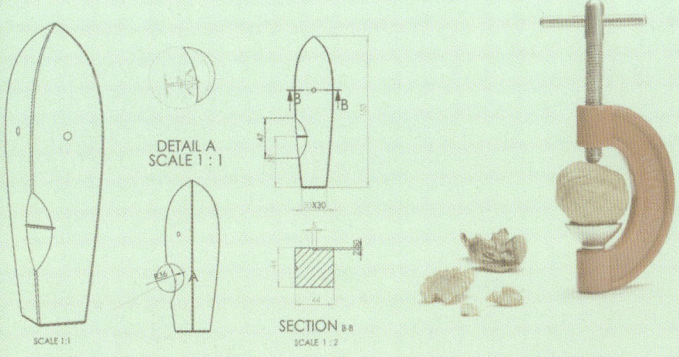
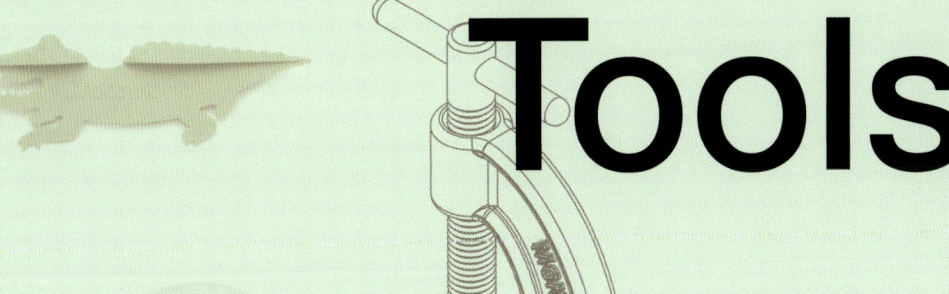

Tools

Unbalance

"The tiniest impact, even a breath of air, is all it takes. Once triggered, the rhythmic motion spreads inexorably to the outermost parts, then slows back into stillness. There is nothing mechanical about the motion of this contrivance. We see the restoration of a natural balance, momentarily upset. The driving force is inertia, as with the branches and leaves of a tree, moving in the wind…" Borrowing one of the most apt comments on Calder's kinetic sculptures, we present Unbalance, the new design by Alessandro Zambelli for Secondome Design Gallery.

Designer: Alessandro Zambelli

Airpouf

It's a hard life for vacuum cleaners: although they are essential electrical appliances, they can hardly be considered as pleasant items. They are often heavy to move, very noisy, bulky and extremely unattractive. Lorenzo Damiani has worked on their substance and shape to create Airpouf. By adding some fantasy to their function, he has redesigned the best technology and wrapped it up in soft and lively materials. He has succeeded in transforming a difficult object into a clever piece of furniture, round and comfortable, movable and ready for anything: it can be both a pouf to sit next to the sofa and a cleaning wizard ready at all times.

The soul of Airpouf hides a 1700 W electrically powered vacuum cleaner in steel and resin provided with a hose and with interchangeable accessories. The pouf in which it rests is padded with cold pressed polyurethane foam and is covered in coloured Lycra. The little ball that stops the air valve is a playful symbol, a little bit magical as well: when the vacuum cleaner is on, it starts floating in the air with a surprise effect. Dedicated to those who still have the eyes of a child.

Designer: Lorenzo Damiani for Campeggi Srl
Photography: Lorenzo Damiani

Juice Bruce

You might be fooled by Bruce's good looks, but he is not just eye candy!

There is nothing that Bruce enjoys more than juicing citrus fruits. Head first he goes – into the lemon, orange, grapefruit twisting and turning until every last drop has been extracted.

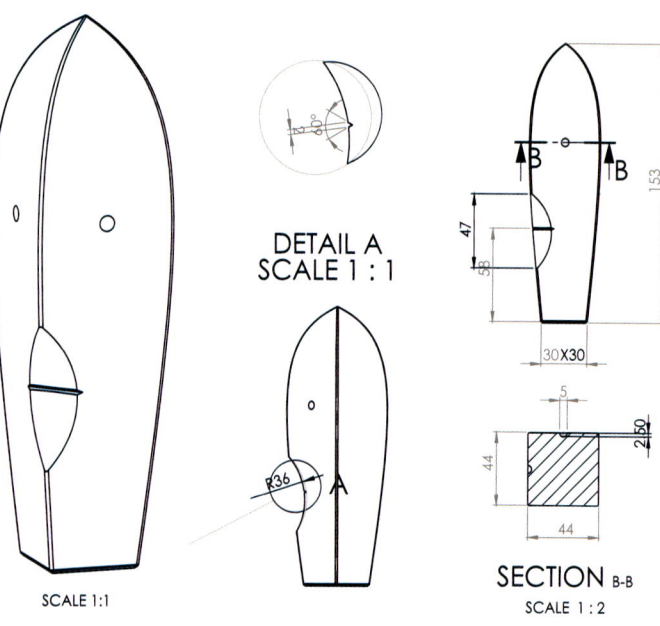

Design: Studio Yaacov Kaufman for Monkey Business

○ A Collection of Creative Furniture and Household   187

Fitcut Curve

The scissors with newly-developed "Bernoulli Curve" blades which maintain the ideal blade angle (30 degrees) throughout the cutting range. With three times the cutting quality compared with conventional scissors, it steadily holds objects and easily cuts not only paper sheets but also corrugated cardboard sheets, PET bottles or milk cartons.

The low rebound grip using thermoplastic Elastomers around finger rings also reduces the burden on hands and fingers.

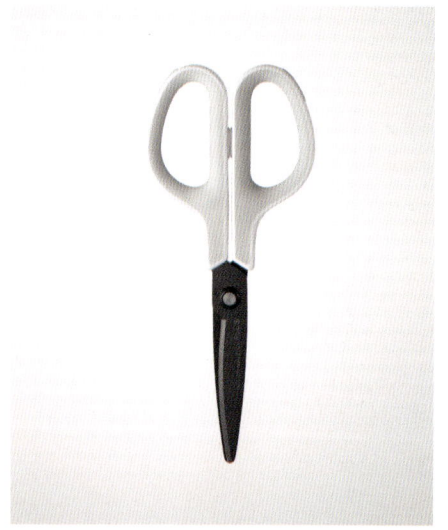
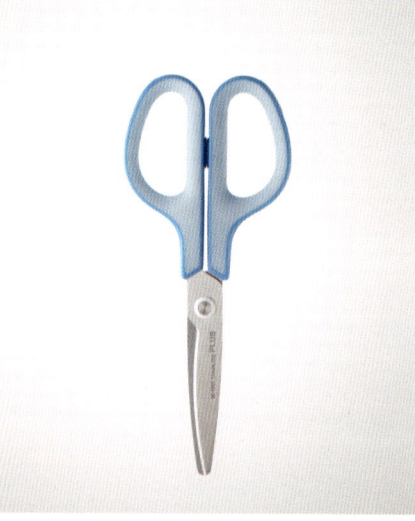
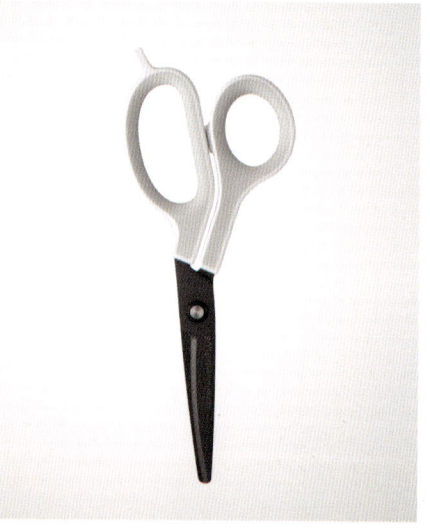

Designer: Ichiro Iwasaki

Biscut Cookie Cutter

This unique cookie cutter will turn dough into delicious cookies or crackers with no waste at all. Just roll it on the flattened dough to create breaking marks, bake it, brake it - and you're done! Easy to bake, fun to break!

Designer: Peleg Design

◎ A Collection of Creative Furniture and Household

Write on

For creative decorating of cakes, cookies, pancakes & more.

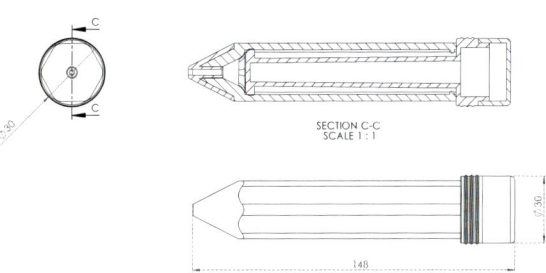

Design Agency: Avichai Tadmor for Monkey Business

Nutwork

A Nutcracker that takes inspiration from the workshop of many handymen and artisans.

Unlike most nutcrackers this design enables a more controlled cracking of the nut with a slow, gradual turn of the screw.

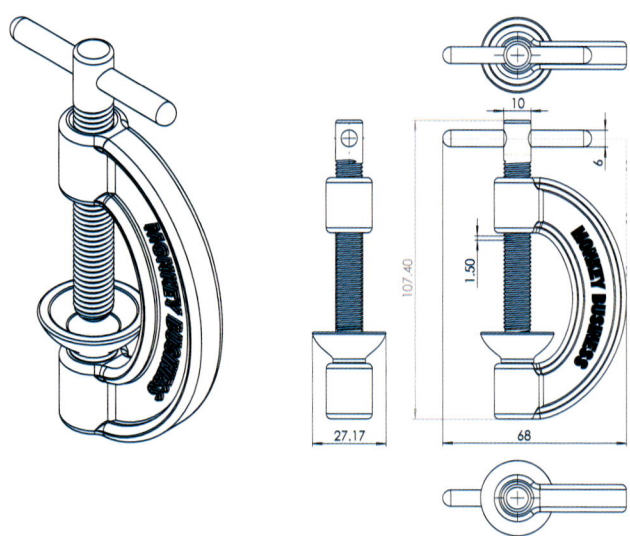

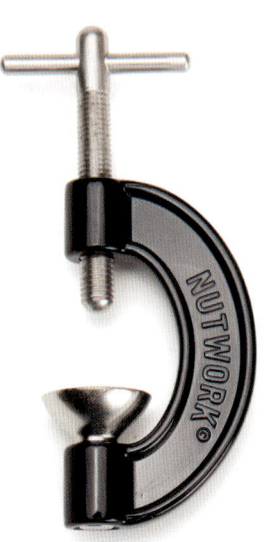

Design: Studio Yaacov Kaufman for Monkey Business

Cooklet Kitchen Tablet Stand

Cooking becomes much easier with this handy tablet stand.

Now the recipes on your mobile phone, tablet, kindle or other devices will definitely stand out, so you can cook at ease. When done – simply hang it on your kitchen rail.

Designer: Peleg Design

Crocomark Crocodile Bookmark

Look out! Deep between the pages lays Crocomark. This crocodile shaped bookmark will silently wait for the right moment to draw you back into the story.

Designer: Peleg Design
Material: Plastic

YolkFrog Egg Separator

Kissing this frog won't turn it into a prince, but with just a squeeze, it will do wonders with eggs. It can easily separate the yolks from the whites – and that's no fairytale!

Designer: Peleg Design

Hardanger Grinder

The Spice Grinders are designed to be functional and aesthetic on the shelf, for cooking and for placing on the table. I guess everyone have experienced pepper corns floating all over the kitchen when you're trying to refill the grinder… This is solved by making a funnellike opening on the top, covered by a soft lid – which also gives a nice grip.

Designer: Per Finne
Photography: Per Finne

Wood Tools

Basic wood tools for food preparation including spatula, ladle, skimmer and rice paddle (shamoji).

The tools are shaped in a way that makes them a natural extension of the hand and to make a good visual and tactile aesthetic experience.

Designer: Per Finne
Photography: Per Finne

Children's Furniture

Bun Van

The Bun Van is a bed, reinvented by Circu. This bed is perfect to bring some fun and imagination to rooms! Inspired in one of the most iconic and magical symbols of fun and freedom! This is one of the most remarkable vehicles ever produced. Few other vehicles have the ability to turn heads and conjure a spirit of freedom, adventure and open roads. The exterior of this piece is made in fiberglass with chrome plated finishes; the inside is made in palisander wood veneer. Inside it contains several storage compartments, a bed, a TV, a secretary, a mini bar and a sofa.

Designer: André Oliveira
Brand: CIRCU

A Collection of Creative Furniture and Household

Little BIG chair for MAGIS

Little BIG chair is for kids from 2 to 6 six years old.

In the kindergarten or at home, it is the combination of a comfortable and light plastic shell with sturdy and stable wooden feet.

A simple system allows the chair to be adjusted to three different heights, in order to grow up with the kids.

Design Studio: BIG-GAME

Fantasy Air Balloon

Air Balloon, inspired in the world of adventure. Is the perfect piece for your kids to dream and be happy! This bed can be customized for little girls or boys. When they grew up, this baby nest can be transformed into a teen sofa. With large storage capacities this amazing piece will help parents organize their kids room. The bottom of this piece is made of the best wickerwork techniques. This handmade touch bring a special touch to this piece.

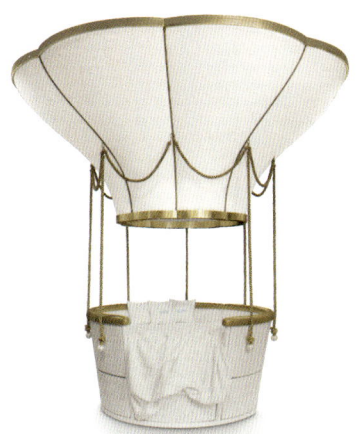
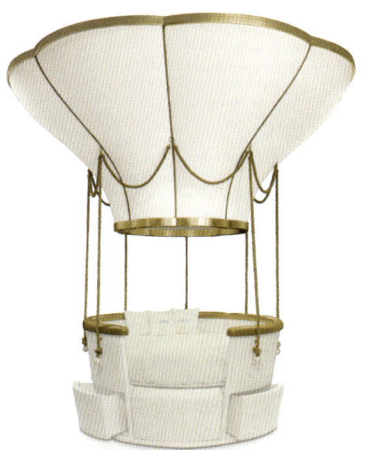

Designer: André Oliveira
Brand: CIRCU

Mermaid Bed

The bed Little Mermaid it's a shell shaped bed. Shells are meant to protect little pearls, to protect them from the Mother Nature. This princess bed will also protect your little girl, and help her to dream and become an undersea princess. This piece is made in fiberglass, nacre painted. Inside, it contains lighting.

Designer: André Oliveira
Brand: CIRCU

Rocky Rocket

Rocky Rocket is a masterpice all made by hand. The body is made in fiber glass, with a masc paint, to reproduce the squares. The interior is made of red velvet upholstery.

It has a light and sound system incorporated. The light and sound system are controlled by a mobile app (Ilight) with several options: choice of music, light effects, and sleep time. The four engines are storage compartments. They are made in fiber glass and their interior, is made with a new velvet flocking technique.

Designer: André Oliveira
Brand: CIRCU

Sky B Plane

Up, up and away! Take off to the sky for some aeronautical adventures. Sky B Plane is a bed inspired by Disney movie "Planes", in which Leadbottom is a puttering old biplane and a grumbling taskmaster. He has too many crops to spray and not enough hours in the day to spray them. For Leadbottom, it's work first, then ... well, more work.

Bring a little aviation-inspired magic to the little pilot's bedroom. With a creative and playful design, the Sky B Plane makes the crib-to-bed transition as painless as possible. The decorative suitcases are storage compartments and allow the kid to climb up and down the airplane. Soar high above the clouds! Some kids are born to fly!

Designer: André Oliveira
Brand: CIRCU

Toy Box Collections

All parents know that extra storage space in their kids' rooms is always useful, and that's why Circu created this valuable Toy Box. The Toy Box family are inspired by the adventures of Scrooge McDuck, the richest duck in the world.

Designer: André Oliveira
Brand: CIRCU

FLY lamp

An essential lamp which is characterised by the "subtle interpretations of the theme". Made in transparent methacrylate, the cover is not perfectly hemispherical but the cut-off is underneath the height of the diameter to collect the most light. What's more, the special transparency of the material and the sheen of the colours bring to mind a soap bubble, iridescent with reflections of light.

Design Studio: Kartell

A comfortable armchair in transparent and colored polycarbonate in the Louis XV style. It is the quintessence of baroque revisited to dazzle, excite and captivate. Louis Ghost is the most daring example in the world of injected polycarbonate in a single mold. Despite its evanescent and crystalline appearance, Louis Ghost is stable and durable, shock and weather resistant and can also be stacked six high. This article has great charm and considerable visual appeal and brings a touch of elegance and irony to any style of home or public area.

Design Studio: Kartell

Bouncer

A resilient wooden base and sculpted plastic shell perfectly support any amount of bouncing your child can create – from the slow and rhythmic to the most erratic and boisterous. Seat and soft harness embrace your child, ensuring safety and comfort with every magical up and down – upright and recline position. A flower screw on the back facilitate cleaning of this sleek.

Designer: Marcel Wanders
Brand: CYBEX

Hausschwein

Let your child's imagination get carried away with this mountable storage domestic pig with removable nose. Lovable in every way, this sturdy plastic animal avails itself for rides as children hold onto its ears as handles while sitting joyously on its back. With an elegantly quilted pattern on its rump, this endearing hog is suited to the most fashionable of home environments. When play time comes to a close, the domestic pig's hollow belly reveals an even greater purpose, storing toys until the next game starts.

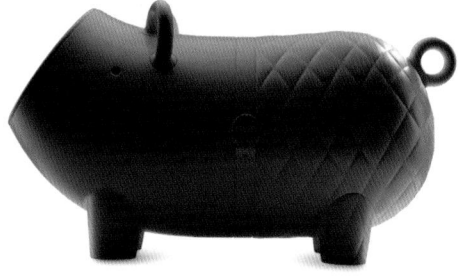
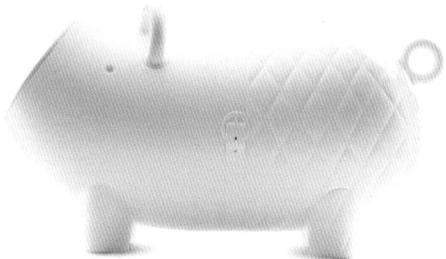

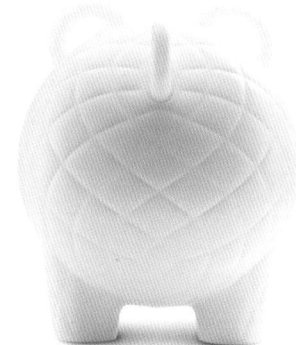

Designer: Marcel Wanders
Brand: CYBEX

Highchair

Make every meal memorable with our iconic wooden highchair, exquisitely designed for comfort and style. Suitable from 6 months up to 3 years (15 kg), the chair is easily adaptable and features a removable snack and play tray and removable safety bar, plus the footrest can be adjusted to the preferred height so your tot will always be comfortable. This outstanding highchair is made from a beech frame, chrome-plated steel parts along with an ergonomic, durable plastic seat shell which supports a luxurious cushion that is lavishly embroidered and attached on the back with an iconic flower screw. Who knew mealtimes could be so stylish?

Designer: Marcel Wanders
Brand: CYBEX

A Collection of Creative Furniture and Household

Rocker

Enjoy moments of bliss when you lay your child in this contemporary reimagining of the classic rocker. The instantly iconic chair, with a solid wooden base and sculpted shell, fit into any stylish home. Its seat becomes the foundation for rest, and its frame provides super-smooth rocking with hardly any effort. A cozy seat coaxes your child to dreamland while a soft harness comfortably cradles it during slumber.

Designer: Marcel Wanders
Brand: CYBEX

Monster Toys

These artful, exquisitely crafted hand puppet collectibles draw imagination and curiosity from every child. Stylish and playful, these monsters captivate, leading us on the most fantastical of journeys.

Designer: Marcel Wanders
Brand: CYBEX

Glücksstuhl

Glücksstuhl is a chair designed with children in mind, age 1 and up. It also functions as a ride-on, a walker with wooden wheels, and a chalkboard. It has a drawer for keeping secrets, and two little eyes for hiding things.

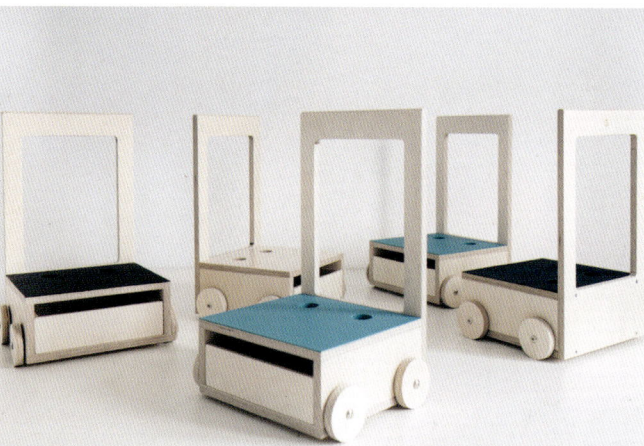

Design: Francesco Monaco
Photography: Jose Luis De Lara

Brand: NIMIO

TOLDINA Mini RC for Kids

TOLDINA* (on the sunny side) is a family of lounge chairs and rocking chairs made of a wooden structure (natural pine or natural beech) and awning fabric in different colours and patterns, and MINI RC for kids is the little rocking chair version for children.

Design: Francesco Monaco
Photography: Jose Luis De Lara

Brand: Nimio

The Walrus Family

The Walrus Family is the family of walruses by NIMIO: two stools and a table for children combining kids imagination with a solid, happy and abstract shape.

THE BIG WALRUS STOOL color is handmade with industrial and resistant birch plywood. Their faces are painted a color each, with 3 combinations that we love. You can immerse in our universe of colors:

As it is not possible to see both sides at the same time it will seem that walruses are changing every time and they will adapt to your needs.

Design: Francesco Monaco
Photography: Jose Luis De Lara

Brand: Nimio

Eames Elephant

Almost no other animal is as popular as the elephant. Admired for its majestic size and loved because of its gentle nature, the elephant is an everyday presence in our lives – as a stuffed toy, storybook figure or heraldic animal. Charles and Ray Eames also succumbed to the pachyderm's charm and developed a toy elephant made of plywood in 1945.

Designer: Charles & Ray Eames
Brand: Vitra

Wooden Dolls

Together with Charles and Ray Eames and George Nelson, Alexander Girard was one of the leading figures of postwar American design. A key source of inspiration for his wide-ranging oeuvre, which focused primarily on textile design, was his passion for the folk art of South America, Asia and Eastern Europe.

Designer: Alexander Girard
Brand: Vitra

Zoo Timers

As a truly multi-talented designer, George Nelson was also successful as a graphic designer. His Zoo Timers – animals drawn in bright colours – offer children a playful and cheerful start to telling the time.

Designer: George Nelson
Brand: Vitra

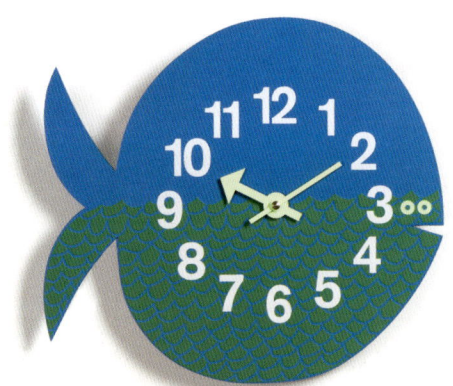

Furia Rocking Horse

Rocking horse with bent beech wood frame.

Upholstered leather seat. Leather details. Standard collection finishes and colours.

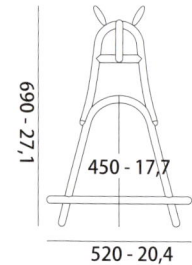
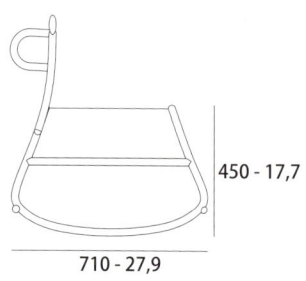

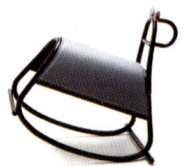

Design: Front for Gebrüder Thonet Vienna GmbH

CONTRIBUTORS

4P1B Design Studio   www.4p1b.com
273 Collection — 006
DEUS Collection — 008
Juice — 009
Revolution — 010
Grapevine — 072
Icenine — 088
Rhapsody Coffee Tables — 089

Alessandro Zambelli   www.alessandrozambelli.it
Lume — 012
Reverb — 028
AtenaSeat and Armchair — 090
Araes Dining Table — 091
Lunapark — 092
Ori Coffee Table — 093
Unbalance — 184

Alexander Lotersztain   www.derloteditions.com
Bolet Wire — 048

Alicja Prussakowska   www.alicjaprussakowska.com
Mizu — 073

Alvaro Catalan de Ocon   www.catalandeocon.com
PET Lamp — 030

André Oliveira   www.circu.net
Bun Van — 202
Fantasy Air Balloon — 205
Mermaid Bed — 206
Rocky Rocket — 207
Sky B Plane — 208
Toy Box Collections — 209

Andrea Ponti   www.andreaponti.com
Kanban — 094

Andreas Kowalewski   www.andreaskowalewski.com
Clamp Chair — 095
FALDA Tables — 096
PIANI Table Range — 097

Arian Brekveld   arianbrekveld.com
Back Me Up — 098
Zoom – In Sofa — 099
Batrang Tableware — 150
Blue Collar Ribbowls — 152

Assembly Room   www.assemblyroom.co.uk
Quayside Pendant Light — 029

BIG-GAME   www.big-game.ch
HAMMER lamp for Wiener Silber Manufactur — 032
SMALLWORK for Habitat — 033
PURE collection for NESPRESSO — 153
Little BIG chair for MAGIS — 204

Bitangra   www.bitangra.com
Amber – Side Table — 076
Amber – Center Table — 100
Hurricane – Bar Stool — 101
Hurricane – Stool — 102
Nucleous – Side Table — 103
Utah Dining Table — 104

Bloondesign   www.bloondesign.com
Springtime — 074

Boca do Lobo   www.bocadolobo.com
Concave Metamorphosis Mirror — 014
Metamorphosis — 015
Robin Mirror — 016
Ann Floor Lamp — 034
Union Table Lamp — 035
Metamorphosis Sideboard — 077
Pixel Cabinet — 078
Aquarius — 105
Empire Center Table — 106

Bram Vanderbeke   www.bramvanderbeke.com
Endless — 037
Stacked — 079
Reinforcements — 080

Campeggi Srl	www.campeggisrl.it	**Ilaria Innocenti & Giorgio Laboratore**	www.1stdibs.com
ABC	107	SELFPORTRAIT hand mirror	013
Gilbert & George	108		
Shelf	082	**Iwasaki Design Studio**	iwasaki-design-studio.net
Nessy	109	PIN	051
Ostenda	110	Cup Table	120
Self – made Seat	111	Fitcut Curve	188
Airpouf	185		
		Jin Kuramoto	www.jinkuramoto.com
Const Lab	www.constlab.ru	Phantom for Smaller Objects	018
MatreshKit — Four-Item Kitchenware Set	181	WIND for OFFECCT	019
		Molly for MEETEE	083
Delightfull	www.delightfull.eu	Liz for MEETEE	084
Atomic Round Lamp	038	Mia for MEETEE	121
Botti Collection	040	Nadia for MEETEE	122
Donna Table Lamp	042	Sally for MEETEE	124
Etta Round Lamp	044		
Hendrix Suspension	046	**Kartell**	www.kartell.com
		FLY lamp	210
EAJY	eajy.de	Louis Ghost chair	211
Beams Chair	112		
		KETTAL / Rodolfo Dordoni	www.kettal.com
Elkeland	elkeland.dk	Kettal Bitta	126
Mirror Mobiles	049		
		Kukka Studio	kukka.co.uk
Filippo Castellani	www.filippocastellani.com	Cubo Light	052
Barlume	017	Felucca Large	053
SILO	155	1141 Table Collection	125
Front	www.frontdesign.se	**Lasvit**	www.lasvit.com
Furia Rocking Horse	226	Fungo Chandelier	054
Gemma Bernal	www.gemmabernal.com	**Leanter**	www.leanter.com
MARTINI	114	Giffy Lamp	055
SASH	115		
		Maison Dada	www.maisondada.com
Giorgio Bonaguro	www.bonagurogiorgio.com	Off The Moon	020
Silhouette	036	Paris-Memphis	022
Medusa	154		
		Marcantonio Raimondi Malerba	www.marama.it
HolmbäckNordentoft	holmbacknordentoft.dk	Palafitt	085
Emma electric kettle	157		
Emma Mugs	176		

Marcel Wanders	www.marcelwanders.com	**NORDI Furniture Ltd.**	www.nordi.com
Bouncer	212	DoRA collection	130
Hausschwein	214	TiME collection	131
Highchair	216		
Rocker	218	**Nueve estudio**	www.n-u-e-v-e.com
Monster Toys	219	Candles	025
		Crockery	158
Mariam Ayvazyan	www.behance.net/sungreen	Kitchen Herb Pot	160
Sun Green Chandelier	056	**O Studio**	orstudio.fr
ENDLESS Light	056	DC1 Chair	132
Mario Alessiani	www.marioalessiani.com	DB1 Coffee Table	133
Antilope	128	DM1 Meridian	134
Carati	129	DT1B White Table	135
Masquespacio	masquespacio.com	**Oeuf**	www.oeufnyc.com
Shade Lamp	057	Brooklyn Desk	136
Massimo Iosa Ghini	www.iosaghini.it	**Peleg Design**	www.peleg-design.com
Concavo Convesso Collection(Volcano)	011	Luma Mobile Phone Night Light	058
KALIKA	050	Babu Toothpick Holder	161
LEVA	066	Oiladdin Pourer & Stopper	162
Concavo Convesso Collection(CHASE tables)	091	Biscut Cookie Cutter	192
KSENIA	116	Cooklet Kitchen Tablet Stand	194
STEALTH Chair	118	Crocomark Crocodile Bookmark	195
STEALTH Stool	119	YolkFrog Egg Separator	196
Monkey Business	www.monkeybusiness.co.il	**Per Finne Design**	perfinne.no
Juice Bruce	186	Miso Bowls	164
Nutwork	189	Naturally Norwegian	165
Write on	190	Wood Containers	166
		Hardanger Grinder	197
Moreno Ratti	www.morenoratti.com	Umami Santoku	198
Collezione Sospesa_Marble Vases	024	Wood Tools	199
NIMIO · furniture looking for people	www.nimio-lab.es	**Phillip Jividen**	www.phillipjividen.com
Glücksstuhl	220	Slant table	137
TOLDINA Mini RC for Kids	221	**photoAlquimia**	www.photoalquimia.com
The Walrus Family	222	Ajorí	168
		Soytun	170
		Titobowl	172

Ponti Design Studio Ltd	www.andreaponti.com	**Studio Roex**	www.studioroex.com

Ponti Design Studio Ltd www.andreaponti.com
Ommo 174

Quentin de Coster - Design Studio
Cloud 059

Richard Yasmine www.richardyasmine.com
Calibre 32 138
Glory Holes 139
Khayzaran / Fairuz 140

Robert van Embricqs www.robertvanembricqs.com
Rising Light Fixture 060
The Rising Chair 142
Rising Table 143

Sander Bakker splinterseed.com
Niki Table Lamp 061

Silvia Ceñal Design Studio www.silviacenal.com
Cowbell lamp 065
Basoa Table 144
Oma Collection 145

Stelton www.stelton.com
EM77 Vacuum Jug 175
Peak bonbonniere 178
Theo Tray 179
To Go Click 180

Stuart Fingerhut stuartfingerhut.com
DROP Pendant 062
Nebula Lighting Sculpture 064

Studio Cheha www.bulbing-light.com
Bulging 2D and 3D Lamps Collection 067

Studio Dessuant Bone studiodessuantbone.com
Collection 22 146

Studio Roex www.studioroex.com
Streamlined Light 031
Streamlined Chair 096
Tubus Beach 147

Vitra www.vitra.com
Eames Elephant 224
Wooden Dolls 225
Zoo Timers 226

WertelOberfell werteloberfell.com
Mannequin Collection 119

Acknowledgements

We would like to thank all the designers and companies who made significant contributions to the compilation of this book. Without them, this project would not have been possible.

We would also like to thank many others whose names did not appear on the credits, but made specific input and support for the project from beginning to end.

Future Editions

If you would like to contribute to the next edition of Artpower, please email us your details to: press@artpower.com.cn